Also available in the series

· J. M. COETZEE'S

Disgrace

ANDREW VAN DER VLIES

continuum

Continuum International Publishing Group

The Tower Building   80 Maiden Lane, Suite 704
11 York Road   New York
London SE1 7NX   NY 10038

British Library Cataloguing-in-Publication Data
A catalogue record for this book is available from the British Library.

ISBN: 978-0-8264-0661-3 (Paperback)

Library of Congress Cataloging-in-Publication Data
A catalog record for this book is available from the Library of Congress.

Typeset by YHT Ltd, London
Printed and bound in Great Britain by MPG Books Group Ltd.

Contents

Acknowledgements

I have benefited enormously from conversations with three gifted readers of Coetzee's work over several years: Lucy Graham, a valued friend, and David Attwell and Peter D. McDonald, generous scholars and colleagues. Other scholarly debts can be inferred from listings in the bibliography. I thank Mark Sanders for reading the typescript, Kathryn Highman for reading a draft of Chapter 2, Angela Wright for vetting my remarks about Romanticism, Gareth Cornwell for sending me material at short notice and Russell Kaschula for advice on Xhosa names. I am also grateful to all the students at the University of Sheffield who have read *Disgrace* with me over the past four years, and to colleagues who have shared their experiences of teaching it.

Without Patrick Denman Flanery's insights, suggestions, comments on the full draft, assistance with the glossary, and unfailing encouragement throughout, this little book would not have been written. My parents have offered ongoing support. This book is for friends and family in the Eastern Cape, but especially for those in

Grahamstown: Sandra and Camel, and Deborah and Timothy, and also their dogs, who have no need of it.

Preface

J. M. Coetzee's *Disgrace* (1999) has, in the decade since its first publication, become both one of the most widely read novels by a South African-born writer, and one of the late twentieth century's most critically acclaimed novels in any language. Only apparently a straightforward realist narrative, its formal complexity and depth of symbolic plotting offers a multi-layered engagement with the politics of writing itself. It is also a rigorous philosophical working out of some compelling ideas about ethics, responsibility and identity in a postcolonial society. Some read it as a bleak account of post-Apartheid South Africa, while for others it is about gender relations and exploitation. For others still, it is a book about the relationship between humans and animals. This short guide will try to suggest that it engages with all of these issues, and more. It is informed by a belief that knowledge of Coetzee's historical and political contexts and his position in particular artistic debates is essential for a fruitful engagement with this demanding text.

I assume no prior knowledge of Coetzee's biography or of his other writing. Chapter 1, The Novelist, introduces the reader briefly to these, offering an assessment of the relevance of Coetzee's other work – including academic and critical writing, as well as fiction and fictionalized memoirs – in the context of Apartheid and post-Apartheid conditions in South Africa, and as a means of contextualizing *Disgrace*. This novel is very much concerned with the limits of European modes of thought, writing and even language, in a once-colonized space: I offer a short account of the longer history of colonial contact, occupation and conflict in the region in the course of Chapter 1, but readers who would like to discover more should consult the Further Reading section at the end of the book. Chapter 2, The Novel, discusses *Disgrace* in relation to a number of significant themes and contexts, and suggests how readers might consider its formal concerns. Chapter 3 assesses the novel's reception, and Chapter 4 discusses its 'performance' in a broader sense, including in literary prize cultures, and as a film adaptation. The final section includes questions for discussion and a glossary, alongside a bibliography.

Quotations from and references to *Disgrace* are to the 1999 Secker & Warburg British edition. Secondary references have been kept deliberately minimal given the nature of this book as a guide, but where I have used them and the source is not clear in context, I give the author's surname (and, to differentiate multiple works, dates) and page numbers in parentheses to point readers to entries in the bibliography.

The Novelist

This section is divided into four sub-sections: a brief biographical sketch, an outline of South Africa's history in order to suggest Coetzee's historical and political contexts, a discussion of his attitudes to writing and politics, and a description of his published work.

Biography

J. M. Coetzee is often described as a notoriously media-shy writer. In fact, he does give interviews, and writes extensively about his intellectual and historical concerns. He is, however, a self-confessedly reluctant interviewee, preferring to write than to speak about his work and his contexts – and there are some things about which he appears not to want to talk (or write) at all. The most illuminating 'interviews' in the public domain are undoubtedly those conducted – incidentally, in writing – with South African academic David Attwell (now a Professor at the University of York), and included in *Doubling the Point* (1992), a collection of Coetzee's essays interspersed with thoughtful interview-like question-and-answer exchanges. They are indispensable for the interested reader, and I draw on them frequently in this guide (using the abbreviation *DP* hereafter).

At the time of writing there was no authorized biography, and many reviews of Coetzee's earlier novels relied on patchy resources, frequently offering divergent accounts of his background (perpetuating confusion about his middle name, among other details). Despite the paucity of authorized information, however, reliable biographical resources (like the Nobel biography edited by Tore Frängsmyr) and information offered by Coetzee himself – especially in *Doubling the Point* and some essays and reviews – do make possible a brief outline of his life.

John Maxwell Coetzee was born in Cape Town, South Africa, on 9 February 1940. He has one sibling, a younger brother. Coetzee's mother, Vera (1904–85), was a primary school teacher. His father, Z. Coetzee (1912–88), served with the South African army during the Second World War in North Africa and Italy during John's very early childhood, and, while a lawyer by training, practised as such only intermittently. Coetzee's parents shared an Afrikaner ancestry, although English was the language spoken at home. Given the complex identifications amongst white South Africans in the twentieth century, it is thus not strictly correct to refer to Coetzee as – or only as – an Afrikaner: 'No Afrikaner would consider me an Afrikaner' (*DP*, p. 341), he has said, English being his first language; nor does he regard himself as being 'embedded in the culture of the Afrikaner' (*DP*, p. 342).

The young Coetzee attended primary school in Cape Town and then in Worcester (a rural town north-east of Cape Town in which the white population was majority Afrikaans-speaking), where the family lived between 1948 and 1951. Coetzee's fictionalized memoir, *Boyhood* (1997), subtitled in its American edition *Scenes from Provincial Life*, deals extensively with the young protagonist John's experience of growing alienation in relation to language, religion and his own cultural interests during this period. This sense would continue: speaking of his late teenage self, Coetzee suggests in *Doubling the Point* that '[s]ociologically, it helps, perhaps, to think of him in his late teens … as a socially disadvantaged, socially marginal young intellectual of the late British empire' (p. 394). Discussing autobiography as a genre, and his own childhood and youth, Coetzee refers to himself here in the third-person, referring to this mode as *autre*biography, the biography of another (an-other; *autre* is French for 'other'). He reiterated this sense that to write about one's younger self was to write about another in a 2002 interview with David Attwell, entitled 'All Autobiography is *Autre*-biography', in which he asked whether the implied 'pact' between the reader and the autobiographer – that there will be 'no outright, deliberate lies' – overrides any desire the author may have to trouble genre definitions or question the 'quite crude definition of lying that many readers may hold' (p. 214). Given these warnings, readers should be cautious about reading either *Boyhood* or its follow-ups, *Youth* (2002) and *Summertime* (2009), as straightforwardly autobiographical: it seems clear that the third, and most likely the first two, contain significant fictions. Nonetheless, Coetzee's *autre*biographies offer useful retrospective comments on the growth of *a* writer's sensibilities in particular historical circumstances, a writer *like* Coetzee and in circumstances like his own, suggesting something of the strong influences on the author's life.

After the family returned to Cape Town, Coetzee, although

nominally Protestant, attended a secondary school run by the Catholic Marist Brothers order, and completed his final year at the end of 1956. He enrolled in the University of Cape Town in 1957 to read for a three-year undergraduate degree, before taking two one-year 'honours' degrees – in English in 1960, and in mathematics in 1961. Between 1962 and 1965, Coetzee worked as a computer programmer in the United Kingdom. (*Youth* narrates the growth of the protagonist John Coetzee's artistic sensibilities between roughly 1959 and 1965, in both Cape Town and London – during the same period, in other words, that the historical John Coetzee was a student in Cape Town and working in London.) Coetzee wrote in an autobiographical sketch published in the *New York Times Book Review* in 1984 (reprinted in *Doubling the Point*) that, after four years of this work, during which even his 'sleeping hours had been invaded by picayune problems in logic', he was 'ready to have another try' at academia (*DP*, p. 50). While in Britain, Coetzee had registered for an MA degree by correspondence (awarded by the University of Cape Town in 1963), writing a dissertation on the English modernist writer Ford Madox Ford. Having secured funding through a Fulbright scholarship, Coetzee subsequently spent three years – between 1965 and 1968 – at the University of Texas at Austin, working towards a doctorate in English, philology and linguistics, and Germanic languages (awarded in 1969). He wrote his dissertation on style in the early fiction of Samuel Beckett: Beckett's prose, particularly his novel trilogy *Molloy*, *Malone Dies* and *The Unnameable*, would be a significant influence on Coetzee's writing.

Coetzee's first academic post was at the State University of New York in Buffalo, from 1968 to 1971. In *Doubling the Point* he suggests that he 'had no desire to return to South Africa' (*DP*, p. 336), particularly as his two children – Nicolas (1966–89) and

Gisela (b. 1968) – had been born in the United States: Coetzee had married Philippa Jubber (1939–91) in 1963; they divorced in 1980. Coetzee applied for permission to remain in the US but it was turned down, and he returned to a post at his alma mater, the University of Cape Town, in 1972, working there, through successive promotions, until his retirement as Distinguished Professor of Literature in 2000. He also held a number of visiting positions between 1984 and 2003 at American universities including Johns Hopkins, Harvard, Stanford and Chicago (where he was a member of the distinguished Committee on Social Thought for six years).

In 2002, Coetzee and his partner, the South African academic Dorothy Driver, emigrated to Australia, where Coetzee holds an honorary research position at the University of Adelaide. In March 2006, he became a naturalized Australian citizen. He has received numerous awards, including the *Prix Etranger Femina* (1985) and the Jerusalem Prize (1987). He became the first writer to win the Booker Prize twice, in 1983 and 1999. In 2003, he was awarded the Nobel Prize for Literature. In 2005, the Republic of South Africa conferred on him the state honour of the Order of Mapungubwe.

Historical and Political Context

Coetzee was eight years old when the Afrikaner-nationalist National Party (NP) came to power in parliamentary elections in South Africa in May 1948 (strictly, the Party was the 'Purified', then the 'Reunited' National Party). He thus grew up in what he calls 'a time of raging Afrikaner nationalism' (*DP*, p. 393), a period dramatized effectively in *Boyhood*. The NP became more notorious, of course, for what came to be known as Apartheid, literally *apart*ness or separateness, a shorthand designation for a complex and pernicious system of laws predicated on the classification of all South Africans in terms of a crude racial hierarchy: white, black (or African – a number of other terms were in use during the Apartheid era, including 'Bantu' or 'native', both of which are now considered offensive), coloured (about which I will have more to say in Chapter 2) and Indian (largely descendants of indentured labourers from southern India). Coetzee explains in an essay in the collection *Stranger Shores* (2001) that 'the basis of the system was ultimately tautological: a white was defined as a person of white appearance who the white community accepted as white, and so forth' (p. 309). Increasingly absurd tests (the curliness of hair, for example) were used to determine race, though the results of this classificatory mania were far from absurd: sexual relations or marriage between races was outlawed, amenities and residential areas reserved for certain races, and re-classification of one member of a family could have serious consequences for the entire family's livelihood, place of residence, and so forth. The Apartheid era ended, after formal multi-party negotiations (conducted in the period following the unbanning of anti-Apartheid opposition parties and release of political prisoners in 1990), with the country's first election under universal franchise in April 1994, and the inauguration of Nelson Mandela as the first democratically elected president of the republic the following month.

It is worth remembering that, although Apartheid denied all non-white South Africans effective political representation or participation in democratic processes, greatly exacerbated inequalities, and was responsible for human rights outrages, it built upon and codified policies of racial segregation and attitudes of supposed racial superiority that were introduced by Dutch and English colonists over the previous 300 years. It was, in some senses, the logical – though no less horrific, tragic and culpable –

outcome of centuries of colonial exploitation. This is why the legacy of violence and racial discrimination has not disappeared quickly: post-Apartheid South Africa continues to bear the scars, and deal with the aftermath, of a long history of brutality and oppression.

The first recorded European visitors to the region had been Portuguese navigators, most famously Bartolomeu Dias (1488) and Vasco da Gama (1492). European settlement began in earnest, however, in 1652, with the foundation, by the Dutch East India Company, of a refreshment station (that would grow into Cape Town) to provision ships making their way to the East Indies (present-day Indonesia). Farmers, their numbers swelled by French Huguenot refugees after the late 1680s, gradually expanded the limits of the colony north- and eastwards throughout the eighteenth century, displacing indigenous peoples along the way. Britain controlled the Cape Colony between 1795 and 1802, and again more decisively from 1806.

In the early nineteenth century, the British colony's eastern frontier expanded, crucially in the area around present-day Grahamstown and Salem (the setting for much of *Disgrace*), where British immigrants were settled in the 1820s to populate a buffer zone with the independent black pastoralist Xhosa people. (Scholarship and public discourse in South Africa now generally uses prefixes in referring, for example, to the amaXhosa people and the isiXhosa language. Coetzee does not use these in *Disgrace*, and the non-South African reader may find them distracting, so I use the form 'Xhosa' throughout.) Settlement and farming, particularly by white people of European descent, has thus been intimately connected with the dispossession of original inhabitants of the land – chiefly Khoisan peoples in the western, and black African groups in the eastern sections of the country: this history of contact, and often violent dispossession, is worth bearing in mind as an important context for *Disgrace*.

Descendants of the original Dutch settlement began, particularly in the nineteenth century, to constitute a distinct community speaking a language that had begun to differentiate itself in colloquial speech from the formal language of the schoolroom and Calvinist Reformed Church. With considerable influence, too, from the creole developed by slaves brought to the Cape in the eighteenth and early nineteenth centuries from the Indian Ocean rim (and particularly south-east Asia, Madagascar and Mozambique), this would form a basis for what, in the twentieth century, would be recognized as a distinct Germanic language, Afrikaans. Although some of these people had begun to leave the borders of the British-ruled colony, by 1838 emigration became more organized and culminated in a concerted exodus, a movement memorialized in Afrikaner national mythology as the 'Great Trek' (*trek* is another South African word that has entered the global lexicon).

By the 1880s, two proto-Afrikaner 'Boer' (meaning, originally, simply 'farmer') republics existed in the interior of South Africa: the Orange Free State, and the South African Republic (or Transvaal). Diamonds were discovered in the northern interior of the region (around present-day Kimberley) in the late 1860s, and gold in the 1880s (around present-day Johannesburg). By 1899, Britain and the Boer republics were engaged in a bitter conflict, the Second Anglo-Boer or South African War, which would end in 1902 in defeat for the Transvaal and Orange Free State. In 1910, they united with two British colonies in the region – the Cape Colony and Natal – to form a white-ruled dominion within the British Empire. Emphasis had been placed in forming the Union on reconciliation between Boer (white proto-Afrikaner) and 'British' (white English-speaking) South Africans, at the expense of justice for the majority of the country's population. Thus, just as Afrikaner nationalism grew steadily throughout the 1920s and 1930s, capitalizing on memories of defeat in the Anglo-Boer war and poverty amongst many Afrikaner communities, so too did black African nationalism, particularly under the aegis of the African National Congress, founded in 1912 – though so named in 1923. It would be the clash between these two entities that would structure much of the country's twentieth-century history.

By the late 1960s, the Apartheid state had imprisoned or forced into exile many of its most vocal opponents (Nelson Mandela, arrested in 1960, was imprisoned for life in 1964) and banned many political organizations. The endgame of the Apartheid state began, in many ways, in the early 1970s, a period of economic crisis, growing internal dissent, and threat from immediately beyond its borders. In 1974, Mozambique and Angola both gained their independence from Portugal, and their new governments proved hospitable to the armed wings of anti-Apartheid organizations (like the ANC's *Umkhonto weSizwe*, 'spear of the nation'). In 1976, students in the large black township of Soweto, outside Johannesburg, rose up against the imposition of Afrikaans as a medium of instruction in schools. By the mid-1980s, the country was in turmoil, with mass action and civil unrest being met with repressive States of Emergency, effectively the national imposition of martial law.

Politics and Art

During the first decade of Coetzee's writing career (his first novel was published in 1974), writers inside South Africa were thus confronted with an increasingly repressive government committing ever-worsening human rights abuses that were difficult to ignore, and which posed challenges for artists and intellectuals. For some, the work of writers who felt that it was imperative first and foremost to report on conditions in the country was no better than journalism. On the other hand, writers offering highly crafted work drawing on European models were accused of irrelevance and irresponsibility. This is how Coetzee's early work appeared to some left-wing critics who thought it too hermetic or oblique, and not sufficiently engaged with the South African socio-political situation. In *Doubling the Point*, commenting on the manner in which he found himself returning to South Africa in the early 1970s, Coetzee remarks that a *'real* resolution would have been to hurl [him]self bodily into the anti-imperialist struggle', although he qualifies this construction: 'I use that language in a spirit of irony; yet what other language is there?' He continues, however, to note that the idea of him 'marching to the fray – I, with my craving for privacy, my distaste for crowds, for slogans, my almost physical revulsion against obeying orders ... was simply comic' (*DP*, p. 337). The comment suggests Coetzee's sense of political urgency, but also his distrust of ideology and orthodoxy of any variety.

What Coetzee did was to write, and to offer in his fiction an unusually sophisticated engagement with these dilemmas; his novels thus remain not only startling examinations of the conditions of thought in Apartheid South Africa, but pertinent to many situations of unequal power persisting in a largely decolonized but nonetheless neo-colonial world. Coetzee's self-consciousness about language and his affinity with philosophical critiques of systems presenting themselves as authoritative or explanatory (in critical terms, Coetzee's affinity might be said to be with certain strands of post-structuralism) were considerably enriched by – and also responded *to* – his contexts as a writer in Apartheid-era South

Africa. In the words of David Attwell (in his 1993 book, *J.M. Coetzee: South Africa and the Politics of Writing*), Coetzee's is 'a fictional oeuvre of unusual complexity... in which narrative discourse and social conflict struggle for authority, in which ethical questions fasten tenaciously to forms of reflexive play that elsewhere seem to have made a virtue of relativism, and in which, finally, the West confronts the limits of its own discursive powers, even its powers of subversion, historicization, and displacement' (p. 10).

Coetzee's principled determination to write on his own terms found unusually forthright expression in comments made at a book fair in Cape Town in October 1987 (later published as 'The Novel Today'). The contexts of the address included Coetzee's ongoing opposition to censorship in Apartheid-era South Africa. He commented on what he saw as a 'powerful tendency, perhaps even dominant tendency' in the country at that time 'to subsume the novel under history'. In this climate, he argued, 'the novelistic text' was construed as 'a kind of historical text', something merely supplementing 'the history text' – in other words offering itself simply as a representation of life under circumstances described in history books (which, of course, are always already ideological) ('Novel Today', p. 2). Such writing, Coetzee noted, would inevitably, in such circumstances, have 'attributed to it a greater truth' than writing which did not; he insisted, however, that he was *not* attempting to distance himself 'from revolutionary art', nor endorsing a sense that 'there is nothing nicer than cuddling up in bed with a novel and having a good old read' (p. 4). Rather, he maintained, art had to have a position from which to speak in its own way, not beholden to any particular politics or positions: to speak only in a manner endorsed by the reigning powers – either institutional or intellectual – would be to have one's work scripted *by* such powers. Coetzee's work has always been more interested in interrogating such powers, and also questioning fiction's own presumed but precarious authority to speak. We see this in Coetzee's use of unreliable narration, foregrounding of textuality, interest in contingent or even structurally impossible occasions of narration, investigations of complicity and violence, and representation of moving – as well as troubling – encounters with 'otherness'. It is worth noting that Coetzee voiced a similar defence of the literary in remarks delivered at the same anti-Apartheid book fair the following year, but never published, in response to the withdrawal by the organizers of an invitation to Salman Rushdie, whose novel *The Satanic Verses* had recently been published in Britain and over which local Cape Town Islamic organizations were threatening violence (see Attwell 2006, pp. 26–7; P. McDonald 2009, pp. 212–14). Coetzee was to return to the issue of censorship and the demands on the literary in a number of essays in his 1996 collection, *Giving Offense*; the essay in that volume on Erasmus, madness, and folly extends and complicates the arguments advanced in 'The Novel Today', and rewards attention.

A Writing Life

The young Coetzee published poems in student newspapers and journals while at the University of Cape Town. *Youth* suggests that he may have made his first attempts at prose fiction while living in London in the early 1960s (pp. 62–3), but it was while living in the US that he began what would become his first published novel, *Dusklands*, which was completed in Cape Town, and published by a small radical press, Ravan, in Johannesburg, in 1974. It consists of two narratives. One is set in the interior of what is now South

Africa in the eighteenth century, narrating the exploits of an explorer, Jacobus Coetzee (a distant ancestor), and drawing on Coetzee's reading – in London and in Austin – of early travel narratives and accounts of the Cape. The other is set in southern California during the early 1970s against the backdrop of the war in Vietnam, and features a propagandist, Eugene Dawn, who works for the American government. Writing of his period in the United States, Coetzee would later reflect that the Americans among whom he lived and worked, 'fine people, generous, likable, liberal in their values', were just as powerless against 'the war machine' in Vietnam as 'liberal whites at home' were to halting some of the brutal actions of the Apartheid government (*DP*, p. 337). *Dusklands* sought to explore the violence implicit in acquisitive or expansionist Western ideologies – early European colonialism in Africa, and American imperialism and anti-Communism in south-east Asia – and to suggest parallels between them.

Coetzee's second novel, *In the Heart of the Country* (1977), the first also to be published abroad (in the US as *From the Heart of the Country*, and in the UK under its original title), returned to similar issues. In 266 numbered sections, it offers the highly unreliable first-person narration of a white spinster, Magda, on a farm in (apparently colonial-era) South Africa. Magda tries to write and rewrite her own story, refusing the imposition of stereotypes or identities by her father, her servants or her sense of her language and its history. Significantly, the South African edition of the novel was published with long passages of Afrikaans dialogue. This novel received wider critical attention, and earned Coetzee the CNA Prize, then South Africa's premier fiction award, in 1977.

Coetzee won this prize again, in 1980, for his third novel, *Waiting for the Barbarians*. This is a third-person, present-tense narration of a period in the life of a Magistrate of a small, fortified town on the outskirts of an unnamed empire. Again, the novel's temporal setting is not explicit, and it can be read as an allegory of the colonial experience, exploring the inter-connected operations of language, ideology and violence in constructing and subjugating an empire's enemies. The Magistrate, who thinks of himself as a liberal man of conscience, finds that he is necessarily complicit with the regime and its acts of brutality, including torture and sexual exploitation. This novel received a great deal of critical attention, and won two significant British literary awards: the Geoffrey Faber Memorial Prize, and the James Tait Black Memorial Prize. Its critical and commercial success facilitated the publication of *Dusklands* abroad, and also the publication of all the novels to date in Penguin paperbacks, through which Coetzee's work began to reach an Anglophone audience internationally. It also began to be translated widely.

Life & Times of Michael K (1983), which won Coetzee his first Booker Prize, was the first of Coetzee's novels to be set in a recognizably modern South Africa – although one not entirely real or contemporary. The novel imagined, from the early years of the decade, increasing civil disorder and unrest possibly culminating in some kind of war, from which a hare-lipped gardener, the eponymous *K* (whose name suggests Coetzee's debts to Kafka), attempts to escape. He tries, with little success, to flee the physical impositions of authority that endeavour to write him into a particular version of history. In the second part of the novel, the reader has access only to the puzzled address, to K, of a medical officer insistent on understanding him, and in effect of writing his story for him. By this point in Coetzee's career as a writer (he had by now established himself as a scholar of stylistics, and a university teacher of literature), his chief concerns had become apparent: explorations of the violence implicit in Western discourses of power, and the ramifications of these discourses for issues of gender, identity and the responsibilities of the writer in unequal societies.

Foe (1986) investigates all of these issues in a creative rewriting of two novels by Daniel Defoe: *Robinson Crusoe* and *Roxana*. Coetzee's novel features a tongueless Friday and a female castaway whose story is stolen by a ne'er-do-well male author. It is the violence implicit in processes of canonization that is at issue here, too. Coetzee would revisit issues of silence, the canon and otherness in *The Master of Petersburg* (1994), a creative engagement with Dostoevsky. *Age of Iron* (1990) takes the form of a letter written by an aging, ill, former classics professor, to her daughter in America, and meditates on death, violence, commitment and otherness: it was the first of Coetzee's novels to be set unambiguously in present-day Africa. The first fictionalised memoir, *Boyhood*, appeared in 1997. *Disgrace* was published in 1999. That year also saw the publication of the 1997–98 Tanner Lectures in Human Values that Coetzee had delivered at Princeton University, as *The Lives of Animals*. The lectures took the form of two fictional narratives featuring an Australian novelist called Elizabeth Costello, who is asked to deliver a lecture at a prestigious college, and offers polemics about the exploitation of animals (comparing slaughterhouses, at one point, to Nazi extermination camps). Both narratives were incorporated into *Elizabeth Costello* (2003), along with other fictions (some delivered as lectures elsewhere) featuring Costello. She appeared, too, as a *deus-ex-machina*-like author in her own fiction, in *Slow Man* (2005), which received mixed reviews. *Diary of a Bad Year* (2007) offers three parallel narratives: one, a series of opinions on politics and art by a writer sharing some (though not all) of Coetzee's life story (the character is the author of a book called *Waiting for the Barbarians*, for example, although other details do not fit with what is known about Coetzee himself); the second his narrative of encounters with a Filipino-Australian woman who lives in his apartment complex and takes on typing for him; the third is her narrative. Coetzee's second fictionalized memoir, *Youth*, appeared in 2002; it was sold in some editions as 'fiction'. Coetzee's third fictionalized memoir, *Summertime*, appeared in September 2009, and further complicates the factual basis of the narrative (in a manner similar to *Diary of a Bad Year*).

Coetzee has also been active as a critic and essayist. *White Writing* (1988) discusses the 'Culture of Letters in South Africa' (its subtitle), specifically in relation to responses to the land by writers owing cultural or intellectual allegiances to European thought and values (hence 'white' writing). *Doubling the Point* (1992) collected early essays alongside revealing interviews on Coetzee's life and work. *Giving Offense* (1996) collected his essays on censorship and literariness in a number of cultures. Two collections of occasional and review essays have also been published, *Stranger Shores* (2001) and *Inner Workings* (2007). Both include many pieces first published in *The New York Review of Books*. Coetzee has also translated Dutch and Afrikaans literature.

2

The Novel

Introduction

Reading *Disgrace* as primarily or *only* about post-Apartheid South
Africa arguably diminishes the novel's power and underestimates
the demands it makes on the reader, as well as the rewards it
offers. However, interpreting it as an examination of themes and
dynamics of power that might be of broader – even universal –
relevance (the resilience of the individual in the face of great
historical turmoil, perhaps, or the damage wrought by unfettered
sexual desire acted on as if by right) is likewise arguably to
diminish the novel's sophisticated engagement with a particular
time and place, post-Apartheid South Africa, and with a long history of oppression in the region. Unsurprisingly, *Disgrace* has invited both readings – the local or particular, and the universal (as I
will discuss in Chapter 3). Readers encountering the novel for the
first time may be bemused either at the hostility, or the praise, the
novel has attracted: it speaks to different readers in different ways,

and to insist on a single interpretation (or agreement on its most important 'message') is in some ways to refuse to remain open to its suggestive complexity.

This chapter is divided into three sections: Issues; Contexts; and Form. In the first, after a brief synopsis, I discuss some of the most obviously significant issues with which *Disgrace* engages, gender and 'otherness' (or, to use a theoretical and philosophical term as shorthand, alterity). These can not readily be disentangled, and are also better understood in relation to some of the most significant contexts I discuss. The latter include race and racial politics in South Africa, the cultural and socio-political resonances of the spaces in which the novel is set (chiefly Cape Town and the rural Eastern Cape), and the European cultural models, specifically those associated with Romanticism, which inform David Lurie's worldview. The final section will turn to consider two other concerns: the novel's engagement with the tradition of the pastoral in the South African context; and Coetzee's interest in the nature of secular confession and the idea of grace (and, of course, disgrace). These formal issues have historical contexts, too, which include respectively the tradition of the farm novel (*plaasroman* in Afrikaans) in South Africa, and the Truth and Reconciliation Commission. Separating out thematic and formal concerns from contextual issues is thus difficult and the reader is encouraged to regard the following sections as an extended and mutually dependent rather than schematic discussion.

Issues

In order to facilitate the discussion of some of the chief thematic concerns of the novel, I offer here a brief synopsis. (This, I should warn readers, makes explicit the plot of the novel.) David Lurie, aged 52 when the novel begins, is a twice-divorced academic feeling increasingly out of place at his university in Cape Town (the Cape Technical University; no such place exists in reality, although it is clearly modelled on the University of Cape Town, where Coetzee himself taught). He is a scholar of modern European languages and literatures but, after major restructuring at the university, is now required to teach courses in communications. He is allowed to retain one specialist seminar, and offers this on Romantic poetry. Walking home from the library one day, he notices a female student, Melanie Isaacs, who takes this class: he invites her to his home, flirts with her, subsequently pursues her, and on their second meeting they have sex. They sleep together on two further occasions. Because the reader only has access to the novel's events through restricted third-person narration (focalized through Lurie) and through Lurie's own words (I will have more to say about this in due course), these acts of intercourse appear less forced than context invites the reader to believe they might appear to Melanie. It seems reasonable, in fact, to assume that at least one of these encounters involves rape. Melanie files a charge of sexual harassment against Lurie and he is called to a meeting and subsequently to a disciplinary hearing at which he pleads guilty to the charges. However, refusing to perform the kind of contrition demanded by the panel, he is forced to resign his post.

Lurie leaves Cape Town to visit his daughter, Lucy, on her smallholding near the small town of Salem in the Eastern Cape, where she runs a kennel for boarding dogs. He volunteers at an animal welfare clinic in nearby Grahamstown, helping a woman called Bev Shaw (with whom he has a less passionate affair than those he is used to). Chiefly, his tasks include euthanizing abandoned dogs and incinerating their carcasses. One day three men arrive on Lucy's smallholding, assault Lurie, gang-rape Lucy, and make off with Lurie's car. Lucy manages to summon help, but later refuses to speak about the incident or lay charges against her assailants. It subsequently becomes clear that Petrus, Lucy's farm manager (to whom she has recently sold part of her land), may know and be protecting the youngest of the assailants. Lurie is frustrated at Lucy's unwillingness to leave the Eastern Cape. Eventually he decides to return to Cape Town.

Lurie breaks his journey in the city of George, home to Melanie Isaacs's family. He meets her father, is invited to the family home for dinner, and there awkwardly asks for forgiveness. Back in Cape Town, he finds that his home has been burgled and ransacked. He tries to work on the chamber opera he has been writing about the Romantic poet Lord Byron's affair with an Italian countess in Ravenna in 1820, although he finds his conception of it changing radically. He attends a play in which Melanie is acting, and is confronted by Melanie's boyfriend. Worried about his daughter, Lurie decides to return to the Eastern Cape for an awkward reconciliation with Lucy, who has reached an accommodation with Petrus whereby he may take ownership of her land in return for his protection. Lucy hopes, too, that he will in time accept into his family the child she will bear: she is pregnant as a result of the rape. David resumes volunteering at Bev Shaw's clinic and, in the final scene of the novel, decides to euthanize a favourite dog.

The novel is everywhere concerned with power, with the relationship between language and authority, and with hierarchies of power in relation to gender, race and historical complicity with injustice. As my brief synopsis makes clear, it is concerned, too, with alterity, both in relation to human relationships and to the non-human other embodied (a term not used lightly) in the novel's representation of dogs and other animals. I will discuss gender and engaging with 'otherness' as key issues; both involve reference to race, which I will discuss under the 'Contexts' heading that follows the thematic discussion.

Gender

For many readers, the novel's key episode is the attack on Lucy and David Lurie in Chapter 11, during which David is set on fire and Lucy is raped. Readers are invariably shocked by this brutal event, and often puzzled by Lucy's reluctance to leave the farm or pursue her attackers. But it is crucial to notice that the novel is concerned with gendered identity, sexual behaviour and exploitation from the very first page. It is also important that everything the reader encounters in the novel is either focalized through the perspective of the character David Lurie (his perceptions), or rendered as free indirect discourse (his words): in other words, while the novel has a restricted third-person narrator, it is clear throughout that the narrative is presented from Lurie's perspective or in his own language. The novel's first sentence makes this clear in the marker 'to his mind' – 'he has, *to his mind*, solved the problem of sex rather well' – and the suggestion that sex is a 'problem' that might be solved (p. 1; my emphasis). What we have here is clearly a self-satisfied character who *believes* that he has a solid grasp of his own existence, but whose delusions and insensitivities are revealed in his very vocabulary.

In relation to Lucy's rape, then, it is important to notice that the event is not described: David is felled by a blow to the head and wakes lying on the floor of the house's lavatory. He *assumes* that Lucy has been raped; when he asks Bev Shaw whether Lucy has had a test for HIV, Bev says merely that he should ask her himself (p. 107). Bev insists that David not draw conclusions or presume to speak *for* Lucy, and reminds him that he was not there, that is to say conscious and in the same room, during the attack (p. 140). Lucy is adamant in her refusal to discuss the attack with her father; she directs him to tell the police what he experienced, explaining that she will 'tell what happened to me' (p. 99). She does later confirm to her father that she has 'had tests' (p. 125), but it is only later still, as they are driving back from Port Elizabeth (where they had hoped to find that the police had reclaimed David's car), that Lurie puts to her directly what he thinks happened, pronouncing 'the word we have avoided hitherto. You were raped. Multiply' (p. 157). Yet this crucially does not capture the experience for her – Lucy's experience cannot be verbalized or adequately represented by David, nor represented for the reader through his point of view; she keeps asking him 'And?'.

What happens to Lucy in the Eastern Cape is not the first instance of sexual exploitation in the novel, although it is certainly the most violent. David Lurie is, however, from the first page of the novel, depicted as exploitative – someone who uses women for his own sexual gratification. He pays at least three women for sex during the course of the events narrated: two prostitutes using the name 'Soraya', and an anonymous 'streetwalker' (at the end of Chapter 21). The first Soraya, the sex-worker Lurie has been visiting every Thursday afternoon for an undisclosed period when the narrative begins, is clearly party to a purely economic relationship, although Lurie misinterprets their encounters as offering emotional as well as sexual intimacy. It is through his focalization that the reader learns that 'they make love' (p. 1); Lurie thinks that Soraya is 'lucky' to 'have found him' and that what he casts as his 'affection is reciprocated' (although, crucially, this observation is qualified by the third-person narration: 'To some degree, he believes' (p. 2). When he happens upon Soraya (and her two children) in the city centre, Lurie's self-delusion leads him to make eye contact, and this seems to change the nature of their encounters: she calls them off, he tracks her down, and she reacts angrily. After the termination of their arrangement, David sleeps with another prostitute (also working under the name Soraya), arranged by the escort agency that arranged the first Soraya, and then sleeps once with a new department secretary at the university, Dawn (pp. 8–9), after which he ignores her.

David constructs excuses for his behaviour throughout the first chapters of the novel: he is shown to think about how his desire is an aspect of his 'temperament', a word that is repeated seven times in the space of a page (p. 2) and anticipates the image of a dog learning to hate its own desire (in the story David tells Lucy on the farm, immediately before the attack [p. 90]). It also anticipates his repeated claims to have been acting as 'a servant of Eros', of some dimly imagined god of desire (p. 52), in pursuing his student. His construal of his own 'temperament' is framed by references to Soraya's that are very clearly his interpolations of her thoughts and feelings, to which he has no access, but which he nonetheless feels certain he is able to discern: she is 'rather quiet, quiet and docile' (p. 1); 'at the level of temperament her affinity with him can surely not be feigned', he thinks (p. 3). In Chapter 2, David tells Melanie that 'a woman's beauty does not belong to her alone', that she 'has a duty to share it' (p. 16). This sounds very much like a sexually predatory heterosexual man's argument for an entitlement to expect sexual favours from any woman he finds attractive.

It is this assumption that women should share their beauty, by which Lurie means make themselves available for sex, which marks him as 'a womanizer', an appellation to which he assents privately (p. 7). He has been married and divorced twice – first to Evelina, a Dutch woman and Lucy's mother (p. 161), then to Rosalind, with whom he meets twice in the novel (and who comments on the 'peccadilloes' that cost him his job and tarnish his reputation [p. 189]). Lurie picks up women at 'the Club Italia' (p. 7), he remembers sleeping with a young German hitchhiker (p. 192), and, of course, he pursues a very much younger woman, his student, Melanie. The first time she comes to his house, he thinks she offers what he interprets as a 'perhaps even coquettish little smile' (p. 12). He offers her a local wine called 'Meerlust' (see glossary), which can be heard as *mere lust*, an ironic authorial comment on Lurie's desire. Of their first sexual encounter, as of his engagements with Soraya, Lurie thinks that 'he makes love to her', but she is described as being 'passive throughout', afterwards averting her face and leaving swiftly (p. 19).

Lurie and Melanie have sex three times altogether. She is said not to 'resist' during their second encounter, but does 'avert herself', and while Lurie thinks this makes the act of intercourse 'not quite' rape, he senses that it is nonetheless 'undesired to the core'; it is as if she died 'within herself for the duration ...' (p. 25). Readers are clearly able to infer from this description, focalized through Lurie, that Melanie is an unwilling sexual partner, that she has perhaps been raped – critics like Lucy Graham (2002) and Rosemary Jolly concur with this interpretation. The third encounter is admittedly more problematic in this interpretive framework: Lurie thinks of Melanie as 'greedy for experience' (p. 29). He may be deluding himself (we should recall that it is *his* impression of the event that is narrated), though he is prepared to admit that he is exploiting her: if she has behaved badly in demanding that he let her stay one night, he thinks, then 'he has behaved worse' (p. 28).

During their conversation on her first visit to Lurie's home, while he invokes Wordsworth as his muse (I will have more to say about Romanticism below), Melanie says she has enjoyed studying Adrienne Rich, Alice Walker and Toni Morrison (p. 13), writers who engage with gender and sexuality. Walker and Morrison, furthermore, are concerned with *race* and gender exploitation. This is a textual clue for the reader unlikely to intuit that Melanie is, in the parlance of the Apartheid era discussed in the first chapter of this guide, coloured. Farodia Rassool, a member of the disciplinary panel before which Lurie is summoned, charges him with ignoring 'the long history of exploitation' in which his actions participate (p. 53), and insists that 'the wider community' has an interest in his contrition (p. 50). Both statements, from the mouth of a woman of colour (her name suggests Rassool, like the first Soraya, would likely have been classed as 'coloured' in the Apartheid era), encode an accusation that Lurie is not only guilty of serious professional misconduct (in sleeping with a student, in falsifying her attendance and academic record), but, in the broader South African context, that he is also guilty of perpetrating – and perpetuating – white-on-black exploitation. The student 'Coalition Against Discrimination' that is demonstrating on campus during the rape awareness week that coincides with the run-up to Lurie's disciplinary committee hearing also alerts us to this concatenation of race and gender issues (see pp. 43, 48).

Lurie remains insistent that he acted on impulse, though not necessarily an 'ungovernable' one (p. 52), in sleeping with his student (or raping her). It is arguably only after his daughter Lucy's rape, and in the face of her insistence on taking ownership of her own story (on not being spoken for, as the focalization has made clear he attempts to do for Soraya and Melanie), that he begins to realize that his actions might be said to exist on a continuum with those of his daughter's attackers. Lucy asks him whether having sex with 'someone strange' is 'a bit like killing' (p.

158); we might recall the sense Lurie has that it is as if something in Melanie dies after the second, undesired, act of intercourse. Lucy also suggests, in a moment of anger and frustration, that her father, as a man, 'ought to know' with what hatred and violence the sex act is able to be carried out (p. 158).

Lucy Graham, who has written perceptively on the representation of rape in the novel in the context of South African politics and culture, also suggests that Melanie and Lucy's names echo two notable rapes of women in the canon of Western literature: Philo*mela* (compare *Mela*nie) in Latin poet Ovid's *Metamorphoses*, and Lucrece in Shakespeare's 'The Rape of Lucrece' (2003, p. 439). Coetzee is a highly allusive writer, and *Disgrace* is one of his most allusive texts: the narrative of Byron and his mistress, Teresa Guiccioli, which David is intent on setting to music as a chamber opera, suggests that narratives of the silencing of women in the canon of European literature is an important concern of his novel. Coetzee had earlier engaged with the issue in his second novel, *In the Heart of the Country*, in which the character Magda wonders what kind of European, metropolitan novel she might have inhabited, and in his fifth novel, *Foe*, which stages the narrative of Defoe's *Robinson Crusoe* as that of a woman, Susan Barton (Coetzee is also referring to Defoe's novel *Roxana*), whose story is effectively taken from her by a male author, Foe (Defoe's original patronymic). Coetzee's re-telling of the Crusoe story is alluded to in *Disgrace*, when David thinks that he would 'not wish to be marooned with Petrus on a desert isle', which is what *Foe*'s island becomes (p. 137). I will have more to say about the canon and Lurie's reliance on references to European literature later.

After Lucy's rape, David, outraged at being considered an outsider by his daughter and by Bev Shaw, wonders whether they think no man capable of empathizing with a woman's experience of sexual violation (pp. 140–1). He asks Lucy whether she wishes to make him think of 'what women undergo at the hands of men' (p. 111). In fact, from his arrival on his daughter's smallholding in the Eastern Cape in Chapter 7, Lucy is shown to encourage David to confront his own solipsism, self-justifications, excuses and delusions. The fact that she is apparently 'lesbian' (p. 105) confounds his understanding of women's beauty in his sense of an economy of desire – and more significantly, heterosexual male desire and sexual gratification – according to which he has always imagined he had a right to act. He notes to himself that she is 'lost to men' (p. 76), and wonders whether her rapists had targeted Lucy because of her sexual orientation (p. 105).

When David quotes English poet William Blake's injunction that one ought to act on one's desires, Lucy offers a rejoinder: she hopes that David does not imagine that his attentions have made the women with whom he has slept better people (p. 70). She suggests that her comments have been made in jest, but the criticism is well directed, particularly given David's continued self-justification (and in particular his construction of his sexual encounters as enriching, in Chapter 21; see p. 192). David offers Lucy the explanation he offered the disciplinary panel, that his 'case rests on the rights of desire' (p. 89), but he realizes immediately that his earlier construction – that he was '*a servant of Eros*' – sounds hollow: 'that is what he wants to say, but does he have the effrontery? *It was a god who acted through me.* What vanity!' (p. 89). Lucy is also reluctant to read a moral into David's story of the male dog who learned to hate its own nature after being beaten every time it sensed a female dog in heat nearby; she asks whether this means that 'males must be allowed to follow their instincts unchecked? Is that the moral?' (p. 90). In both cases, David appears to begin to apprehend the irresponsibility of his own actions, to see that his explanations draw on an understanding of the world based on a selective engagement with European Romanticism that works itself out as an endorsement of solipsism and self-aggrandizement.

Lucy calls into doubt the value of all of the specifically European modes of artistic or linguistic expression that are the touchstones not only of David's career, but his worldview: she jokes with him that he must think her activities – running a boarding kennel and growing produce for a farmers' market – worthless, that he must think she 'ought to be painting still lives' or learning Russian (p. 74). Where David stresses the apparent rights of individual desire, of self-expression, of a concern with individual consciousness and its apprehension of the sublime, Lucy emphasizes individual responsibility and responsibility to others – including non-human others (as will be discussed below). In the wake of Lucy's insistent calling into question of the models by which he has measured his experience of life, David thinks about a painting he has seen reproduced in a book: *The Rape of the Sabine Women*. This depicts an episode from the legend of the founding of Rome, described by Livy and Plutarch, in which the Roman men kidnap women from the neighbouring Sabines. He does not specify which of the several extant this might be, though it is likely, from his description, to be one of the versions by Nicolas Poussin (1594–1665), probably the 1634–35 version in the Metropolitan Museum of Art in New York. Contemplating it in the wake of what has happened to his daughter and everything about which he has been prompted to think, David realizes how the act of rape – or its inference – is rendered aesthetic. He is moved to acknowledge the brutality of the event depicted (or, rather, elided), precipitating a remarkable moment in which he finds he can think himself into the place of the rapists – 'he can, if he concentrates, if he loses himself, be there, be the men, inhabit them, fill them with the ghost of himself' – but is not sure whether he is able to empathize with the women: 'does he have it in him to be the woman?' (p. 160).

This experience prompts David to wonder about the ethics of his own engagement with the story of Byron and his jilted lover, Teresa, the Contessa Guiccioli. He realizes that many of the women Byron would have counted as conquests would have 'called it rape' and that, given his own changing apprehension of the nature of sexual exploitation (and certainly 'from where Lucy stands'), Byron appears 'very old-fashioned indeed' (p. 160). Two issues are raised by this realization that remain to be considered in this section: firstly, how this growing sense of complicity in exploitation plays itself out (specifically in relation to the opera, and, I suggest, in David's relationship to Bev Shaw); and secondly, whether or not David does, in fact, undergo significant change as a character, particularly in respect of his attitudes to gender.

Bev Shaw does not make a favourable impression on David when they first meet: he thinks her a woman who makes little 'effort to be attractive' (p. 72), scorns 'animal-welfare people' (whose unrelenting cheerfulness makes one 'itch to ... kick a cat', he says) (p. 73), and looks down on her straitened circumstances (David is an inveterate snob, as his later attitude to the Isaacs family reveals on p. 170). However, Bev's concern for the animals at the clinic clearly makes an impression on him: we are invited to infer a comparison between the sick goat with an infested scrotum (in Chapter 10) and David (even though he questions the suitability of the term 'scapegoat' in a secular age, and contests its application to his case, on p. 91). Bev comes to minister to David rather as she does to the goat; he later recalls her 'nuzzling the old billy-goat with the ravaged testicles ... comforting him' (p. 126) just as she 'nuzzles' David during their first sexual encounter (p. 149). Their sex is not obviously exploitative, although it is adulterous. Bev appears to be in control, and makes sure that David has a condom – although it is telling that it is through David's focalization that it is identified as a 'contraceptive': Bev is surely past child-bearing age, and while David had worried about Lucy contracting HIV (p. 106), he is clearly not thinking about his own risk of being or becoming a carrier of the virus (p. 149). David thinks afterwards of having 'been succoured' by the act of intercourse with Bev (p. 150). She is, in other words, a woman not obviously attractive in the terms David has previously recognized, yet he finds himself able to engage in a more mutually conducted sexual relationship with her than he has managed during the space of the narrative.

The novel suggests a link between this relationship and David's re-visioning of the character of Teresa in his chamber opera. In the penultimate chapter of the novel, after Lucy has intimated that his return to the smallholding will cause unmanageable tension with Petrus and his family (including Pollux, the youngest of the attackers), David thinks about Teresa. She is, he thinks, perhaps 'the last one left who can save him' (p. 209). Initially, he had planned the opera to be about the young Teresa and the 35-year-old Byron, about to leave her to set off for Greece (p. 162). But on the smallholding, and then when back in Cape Town, he finds 'something misconceived' about the whole project (p. 181), and 'tries another track [sic]': one featuring a middle-aged Teresa, long after Byron has left her, asthmatic, trapped with her aged father and her long-dead lover's letters. Is he able to empathize with *this* Teresa sufficiently to compose music for her, he wonders (p. 182). Bev is an incarnation of the kind of woman David feels he must now find it within his powers to love. If he can no longer have the younger Melanie, if the 'passionate young' (p. 180) Teresa – she is 19 in his original plan for the opera (p. 182) – must make way in his opera for the 'dumpy' older woman with 'heavy bust', 'stocky trunk' and faded complexion (p. 181), then he must also love Bev, who is not unlike this older Teresa.

If Bev is identified with Teresa, one might argue that David finds it 'in his heart to love' both women cast as 'plain' and 'ordinary' (p. 182): Bev is also 'of middle age' and described as a 'plain little creature' (p. 148). And yet even the older Teresa, as imagined by David, refuses to submit to despair or abjure her passionate nature, her 'immortal longings' (p. 209). If we read David's striving after a way of representing undying passion, a nature that refuses to surrender (we might read these as descriptions of David's infatuation with Melanie as much, perhaps, as of Teresa's with Byron), then the opera's increasing absurdity – its music is reduced to '*Plink-plunk*' sounds on a banjo (p. 214) – might equally be taken as the novel's judgment on the futility of this unreconstructed mania. David is shown to think that he is, in fact, 'failing' his vision of Teresa: he is incapable of producing 'a single authentic note of immortal longing' (p. 214), although he seems determined to remain devoted to trying.

The question thus arises whether or not David's attitudes to women change over the course of the novel. Do his attitudes to his own desires evolve to any noticeable degree (insofar as readers are given access to the character's thoughts sufficient to judge)? In some ways, this question is impossible to answer without engaging with the question of what the title might mean, and how Coetzee might be said to be figuring the condition of 'disgrace' in which Lurie regards himself as languishing (pp. 85, 172). The reader has ultimately to decide – but I point to two episodes following Lurie's decision to leave the smallholding in Chapter 18, and preceding his return to the Eastern Cape in the final chapters, which suggest that he appears to continue to experience desire in a similar manner to that at the beginning of the narrative (what he does to ameliorate or atone for such desires will be considered in the following section). In Chapter 19, when Lurie visits the Isaacs family in George, he experiences a flash of desire for Melanie's school-age younger sister, Desiree, and fantasizes about being in bed with both of them ('an experience fit for a king', he thinks [p. 164]). Back in Cape Town, while watching *Sunset at the Globe Salon* (the play in which Melanie is performing, in Chapter 21), he muses on all the women with whom he has slept and thinks about how they have 'enriched' his life (p. 192) before paying a prostitute for sex (pp. 194–5), crudely, enriching her (monetarily, if not emotionally), in the encounter.

'Otherness'

The Swedish Academy's press release – retained on its website – announcing on 2 October 2003 the award of the Nobel Prize in Literature to Coetzee, drew particular attention to the fact that his work frequently 'portrays the surprising involvement of the outsider'. Outsiders have long figured in Coetzee's writing: the barbarian girl in *Waiting for the Barbarians*, the tongue-less Friday character in *Foe*, and the homeless man called Vercueil in *Age of Iron* are only a few, if perhaps the most memorable. For Coetzee's protagonists (the Magistrate, Susan Barton, and Mrs Curren, respectively, in the novels just mentioned), engaging with the marginalized heightens or foregrounds their culpability and complicity in particular systems of oppression. It requires of them acts of generosity that cannot be reciprocated, acts that must be offered without thought of recompense or reward. In *Age of Iron*, Mrs Curren enunciates this concern as being about care, which she identifies as 'the true root of charity', saying of Vercueil: 'I look for him to care, and he does not. Because he is beyond caring ... and beyond care' (p. 20). In *Disgrace*, when David Lurie first balks at Lucy's suggestion that he help out at Bev Shaw's clinic, because such volunteering 'sounds suspiciously like community service', Lucy reminds him that the animals 'won't care' (p. 77). It seems clear, then, that the novel suggests that David comes to sense that it is through negotiating an ethic of responsibility towards animals (and towards their deaths) – displaying a kind of care – that he can find a way, if not exactly of atoning for wrongs (he tells Lucy during the same exchange that he is 'not prepared to be reformed'), then of attempting to work through the state of 'disgrace without term' (p. 172), without end, into which he feels himself to have fallen.

There are intimations of an ongoing concern with responsibility to others from the first chapter of the novel, however. The novel's first suggestion that David will have to engage with the gaze of others (in the philosophy of Emmanuel Levinas, with which much recent discourse about responsibility to others has been concerned, it is this gaze that is of particular importance), comes after he sees Soraya, and the children who accompany her and who he assumes are her sons, in central Cape Town. Thereafter, he imagines these children as 'presences' in the room where he and Soraya have their weekly encounters; they are 'shadows in a corner of the room', whose eyes (he thinks) 'flicker over him covertly, curiously' (p. 6). They make him think, significantly, of the women in his life ('mistresses, wives, a daughter', p. 7), those on whom he feels he has claims, but for whose claims on him he has not adequately accounted. Later, after rumours that David has slept with Melanie become public, her boyfriend shows up in his class on Byron, and 'a dogged silence' settles 'around the stranger' in the class (p. 32).

Dogged knowingly (perhaps even wittily) foreshadows the way in which alterity and dogs come to be connected.

The trope of a stranger in the midst of apparent familiarity recurs, too. At the party to celebrate Petrus's acquisition of part of Lucy's land, the youngest of her assailants, Pollux, is, as far as Lucy and David are concerned, a stranger at the feast (see p. 133). There is also a complex intertextuality at play here: the critic and writer Zoë Wicomb (2002) has elucidated Coetzee's likely reference to Cicero's story of the Art of Memory (involving references to Castor and Pollux, and strangers at a feast) in this episode. And, of course, David, on his return to the party, feels himself the 'stranger, the odd one out' (p. 135). He reprises this role at the awkward dinner with the Isaacs family in George, during which he imagines how he must appear to Melanie's sister, Desiree, as 'the unwanted visitor, the man whose name is darkness' (p. 168). This description connects David to Lucifer, the fallen 'dark angel', a 'stranger' and 'thing of dark imaginings' in Byron's poem *Lara*, which the class discusses in Chapter 4 (p. 32). It also suggests a connection to the (literally dark) 'strangers' (p. 94) who perpetrate the attack in Chapter 11. Derek Attridge (2000, p. 112) suggests that these strangers might be regarded as operating like the *arrivant*, the unexpected guest always wholly and unpredictably other, in the philosophy of Jacques Derrida. We might read the juxtaposition of their description as 'unknown assailants' with the name of the (real) newspaper in which the attack is reported, the (*Eastern Province*) *Herald* (p. 115), as the narrative's endorsement of this view of their purpose.

However, it is undoubtedly the otherness of animals that is central to the novel's engagement with this issue, and to many readers' experience of the novel. Lucy avers that 'there is no higher life' associated with art, or philosophy, or attachment to European ideas: rather, she suggests, there is only one life that 'we share with animals' (p. 74). By the time *Disgrace* appeared in print, Coetzee had recently dramatized a long-standing interest in the manner in which representations of animals engage with the means by which people measure their own status or ethical standards. This was one of the subjects of his 1997–8 Tanner Lectures at Princeton University, published as *The Lives of Animals*, and later incorporated into *Elizabeth Costello*. (In its wake, scholars have looked back at the whole catalogue of Coetzee's work, finding a significant engagement with animals in all of his novels.) David develops from being 'more or less indifferent to animals' (p. 143), to being tremendously affected by their fates. When he learns about Bev Shaw's work at the animal welfare clinic, he finds it 'hard to whip up an interest in the subject' (p. 73). Soon, however, he forms an attachment to an abandoned bulldog, Katie, on Lucy's smallholding, and falls asleep next to her in her cage one day, in a scene inviting juxtaposition with other scenes of David sleeping with female characters: it is metaphorically non-intrusive, and without expectation of return. It also presents a more affirming and humble affiliation with dogs than his comparison with the Kenilworth dog in the story he is yet to relate to Lucy.

David later feels a 'bond' with the two sheep Petrus buys to slaughter for the party, and is concerned at Petrus's treatment of them. The bond is, however, 'not one of affection' (p. 126) – elsewhere he disavows any sense of sentimentality in relation to his or Bev's work at the clinic (p. 143). Nor is it a bond with the *particular* sheep, he thinks, but rather with 'their lot' in an abstract sense (p. 126); in other words, the lot of two animals treated with neglect and destined for slaughter (at the party, he eats the mutton chops he is handed, clearly taken from the sheep, and decides he has to eat them but will 'ask forgiveness afterwards' [p.

131]). Later, when David voluntarily takes it upon himself to deliver the corpses of euthanized dogs to the incinerator, he tells himself that he is saving their 'honour', that the task is undertaken not for the dogs' sake but in service of his own 'idea of ... a world in which men do not use shovels to beat corpses into a more convenient shape for processing' (p. 146).

It is this care which might redeem him for participating in a '*Lösung*' (pp. 142, 218), a solution, the euthanasia of unwanted dogs, of animals regarded by society as 'superfluous' (p. 142), which he compares with the Shoah or Holocaust, the Nazis' so-called Final Solution (*Endlösung*). Elsewhere Lurie reflects, unkindly, that Bev could be said to 'liquidate' the animals that come to trust her (p. 210). We should be careful not to regard this as Coetzee's comparison: it is made by a fictional character. Nor is Coetzee unaware of the problematic nature of the comparison. His character Elizabeth Costello voices similar comparisons in *The Lives of Animals* (and *Elizabeth Costello*), and is there challenged by a Jewish academic who finds the comparison outrageous. In *Disgrace*, the comparison, focalized through Lurie, is not flippant: it reflects on the wilful ignorance of the community at large about the act of putting down unwanted dogs. They expect someone to take care of the problem and, turning a blind eye to its solution, are as guilty of 'sublimation' (p. 142), the comparison suggests, as war-time German society at large might be said to have been of the horrors of the extermination camps (in other words, it is an attitude towards organized killing that is being equated here, *not* dogs and Jews).

Over the course of the novel, however, just about every character *is* described as a dog. David thinks that he has become a 'dog-man: a dog undertaker' (p. 146). Lucy agrees that the accommodations she makes in order to stay on her smallholding render her 'like a dog' (p. 205) – Peter McDonald (2002) points out that these words are also an allusion to the final words of Kafka's novel *The Trial* (1925), in which K. is executed 'Like a dog' (in the words of his executioner), on which the narrator comments that it was 'as if [the killer] meant the shame of it to outlive him' (quoted on p. 329). Petrus describes himself on first meeting David as 'the dog-man' (p. 64), although his acquisition of land – increasing as Lucy's elective dispossession is effected – allows him eventually to declare himself 'not any more the dog-man' (p. 129). Here the contextual resonance is to the treatment of black South Africans under Apartheid, and also to the use of dogs – for example by police – against black men. The apparent acceptance by Lucy of the suggestion that similar brutality might now have to be expected by white South Africans is one of the novel's most difficult and controversial elements.

David's abstraction in relation to the corpses of the dogs, that his service is to an idea of the world and therefore to his sense of a world he would like to inhabit (so, ultimately, an idea that is self-interested), only becomes an embodied concern in the final scene, in which David gives up his favourite dog, Driepoot, to be euthanized by Bev at the clinic. We should, of course, be wary of abstraction: as we saw in the discussion of 'gender' and will see in the discussion of Romanticism, David's penchant is for self-justificatory excuses that rely on abstraction. Lucy, who throughout takes aim at David's ideas, declares that she does not 'act in terms of abstractions' (p. 112), but David frames everything in the abstract – even his emotional response to the euthanasia in which he participates, and cruelty to animals, of which he 'disapproves' 'in an abstract way' (p. 143).

How, then, are we to read the novel's final, bleak image of David delivering the crippled dog (wagging its rear, licking David's cheeks) to its death? This act might be interpreted variously as showing David transcend the abstract, or attempting to demonstrate empathy and responsibility to all suffering others, or finally as yet another selfish (self-justificatory) action. Critic Rita Barnard (2007) points to the phrase from Thomas Hardy's novel, *Jude the Obscure* (1895), '*because we are too menny*' (p. 146), which enters David's thoughts as he contemplates his role in killing dogs regarded by society as superfluous (earlier he thinks 'There are simply too many of them' [p. 142]). The quotation is a reference to a note left by Jude's eldest son to explain his suicide and his hanging of two of his siblings. Barnard argues that this reference suggests that Lurie is shown to accept, in his act of giving up his favourite dog, 'the claims of an infinite number of other creatures' suffering in the world (p. 40). However, Lucy Graham argues that Lurie's 'fussiness about the treatment of dog corpses' is ultimately 'self-indulgent': 'he is possibly the only one who benefits' from these attentions (2002, p. 11). The same might be said of the final scene; in 'giving ... up' Driepoot (p. 220), David enacts a presumption of ownership and sacrifices an attachment for the sake of an abstraction.

While David attempts sympathetic identification with animals, the implicit *comparisons* he imagines with non-human creatures invariably serve his own sense of pathos or tragedy. His connection with the billy-goat has been discussed. He also draws a connection between the Kenilworth dog that hates its own nature and the manner in which he thinks he has been expected to apologize for his desire (see pp. 9, 66). But David does also think of his desire for Melanie as predatory, imagining her as a Red Riding Hood-figure 'in the forest where the wild wolf prowls' (p. 168). And the play in which Melanie performs in Chapter 21 is staged in a theatre that served, until recently, as refrigerated warehouse for carcasses awaiting export (pp. 190–1): the inference is that Melanie has herself served as meat for a predatory Lurie. It also arguably serves to highlight the commodification of animals – and women – in (patriarchal) human society. After the attack on the smallholding, David wonders – somewhat problematically – whether, in post-Apartheid South Africa, with '[t]oo many people' and 'too few things', all property 'must go into circulation ... women, too' (p. 98). The staging of *Sunset at the Globe Salon* in a former dockyard meat warehouse ironically foregrounds David's own complicity, then, in something like the 'circulatory system' (p. 98) he imagines in relation to his daughter's rape.

'Otherness' is at work in the novel not only in embodied (even in abstracted but potentially embodied) 'others', but also in relation to the novel's engagement with music, and in its concern with the nature of disgrace. In *Waiting for the Barbarians*, it is in dreams – multiple vivid sequences are described – that the novel's protagonist, the Magistrate, is able to approach a contingent reciprocity with an imagined version of the novel's representative 'other', the barbarian girl. In some ways, we might read this as a suggestion that only another (an-*other*) kind of discourse, one not beholden to the kinds of writing so easily colonized by authority (state, popular opinion and so on), might provide room for resistance, for exploring the kind of world in which the Magistrate would like to live. In *Disgrace*, we have a character not unlike the Magistrate, obsessed with his own desires and a need to justify his own position, and one who, ultimately, is forced to negotiate a more responsible relationship to others. For David Lurie, however, it is not in dreams but in music that he finds another discourse. I have discussed above how David's conception of Teresa changes throughout the novel, reflecting what might be read as some kind of changed attitude towards gender relations (although I have suggested that this might also be interpreted as not such a straightforward trajectory). But it is significant that David's sense of how art functions also changes. He has begun to distrust verbal communication – he finds 'preposterous' (p. 3) the premises of the discipline of communications studies, which he is expected to teach, and he believes that speech originated in song (p. 4). Yet this high-flown and abstract supposition is rendered ironic, just as his reliance on other – chiefly European – modes of expression is emphasized, in the suggestion that he initially has 'no qualms about borrowing' music for his chamber opera (p. 63). Later, when he does begin to write his own music, it is in the bathetic mode, on a banjo he bought for Lucy long ago when they lived in Durban (p. 184, see p. 187). The music takes David by surprise: it is other in the mode of the *arrivant* – 'this is how' art 'does its work!', he thinks: 'How strange!' (p. 185).

Disgrace is likewise a state of being other – other, perhaps, than that which one would like to be. Disgrace is not necessarily the opposite of grace, although acting without grace might lead to disgrace, and disgrace might be said to persist for as long as grace is not extended to the disgraced. And, if we extend Coetzee's description – in an interview with David Attwell in *Doubling the Point* – of grace as a 'condition in which the truth can be told clearly, without blindness' (p. 392), disgrace might be associated with untruthfulness or blindness, not least about oneself. David thinks at one point that Lucy's silence about the rape is linked, somehow to 'his disgrace' (p. 109); it requires truthfulness about his own complicity in sexual violence to apprehend the link. Elsewhere in *Doubling the Point*, Coetzee suggests too that it is attention to the body, or embodied-ness, that might be the closest approximation of (or the best route to) a state of grace (p. 248). We might read in these statements a suggestion of the importance of David coming to view bodies – of all people, but in his case particularly of women, and of animals – as a means to achieve a kind of grace that might end his disgrace. Ironically, being without the physical love of another is linked to disgrace in Rosalind's confusion about Lucy's apparent former lover, Helen, whose name Rosalind misremembers as Grace (p. 187): Lucy is thus also metaphorically, at least in Rosalind's mind, without grace.

Contexts

Race

The first chapter of this guide offered brief mention of South Africa's history of racial oppression and categorization. *Disgrace* challenges South African readers, or readers with knowledge of South Africa's complex history of racism and racial discourse, not to jump to conclusions about the racial identities of characters in the novel. It foregrounds, in other words, the manner in which race is a discursive construct, something which is performed (or imposed, or contested) in ways that complicate any easy and problematic assumptions that someone *is* simply (and only) 'white' or 'black', and so on. So although the novel is in many ways a 'rainbow' novel, depicting characters who might in fact be said to 'represent' a number of races (and ethnicities) appropriate to the 'rainbow' nation that post-Apartheid South Africa was constructed as being after the first multi-racial elections of April 1994, it withholds explicit terms of racial classification for much longer than one might expect, and consciously so.

It is very difficult, when writing or talking about South Africa in the twentieth century, to do so without using racial terms, even if this is sometimes distasteful or runs counter to discourses of racial equality and non-discrimination central to the project of the post-Apartheid nation. Using racial terms in discussing *Disgrace* seems particularly pernicious given the novel's studied attempt to frustrate readers attuned to markers of racial identification, and yet the novel's subject matter dictates that the fact of the continued importance of race in South African public discourse be directly confronted. Thus, the brutal attack on Lucy and David also challenges the reader *not* to construe its representation (it is, as I have suggested, itself elided in the novel and so requires the reader to reconstruct or construe it) as politically incorrect: black men raping white women – Lucy says she thinks two of the attackers '*do* rape' (p. 158) – is a familiar trope in narratives of white colonial panic.

As the discussion of gender above shows, it is difficult to approach exploitation in relation to gender in the novel without considering the longer history of which David's encounters with Melanie are said by one character to be a part. There is a likelihood that some non-South African readers, or those not as familiar with the racial categories that were enforced under Apartheid (and that continue to inform public debate and the performance of identity in South Africa) may not notice, or may misinterpret, the novel's sometimes subtle racial markers. Helen Small provides an example: in her study of old age in literature, *The Long Life* (2007), she describes Mr Isaacs as a 'practising Jew', and implicitly white (p. 223). The name Isaacs does suggest Isaac, the son of Abraham in the Judaeo-Christian tradition, but this is not an uncommon name in the coloured community, and, as I will show, the novel clearly suggests Melanie's identity as coloured elsewhere, something on which all South African critics agree. Whether or not Small's misreading inhibits enjoyment of the novel is a moot point; it certainly means that a reader may think that the novel engages more with one set of issues than with others. This section, then, is offered as a contextualization of the novel's depictions of race, bearing in mind the caveats issued above. I deal first with Soraya and Melanie's racial or ethnic identities, then with the representation of black men in the novel, and finally with the novel's treatment of other racial and ethnic markers (including suggestions that Coetzee may intend us to think David Lurie is Jewish).

The first Soraya, whom we see Lurie visiting on the first page of the novel, is in all likelihood a South African who might identify as being a member of the Malay community – that is, that section of the coloured community that retains its ethnic, cultural and religious affiliations to a distant south east-Asian ancestry. She is Muslim (p. 3); Lurie gives her a present at Eid (p. 5). She has 'long black hair' and, more significantly, a 'honey-brown body, unmarked by the sun' (p. 1). Lurie also imagines that she lives in Rylands or Athlone (p. 3), both 'coloured' residential areas in the Apartheid era (and still predominantly coloured) in the greater Cape Town area.

Readers should not confuse the term 'coloured' with the term 'colored', once in use in the United States to refer to African Americans. In South Africa, the term was meant by the Apartheid state to refer primarily (as Coetzee explains) to 'the descendants of unions between people (usually men) of European (so-called Caucasian) descent and people (usually women) of indigenous African (usually Khoi – the term 'Hottentot' is no longer polite) or Asian (usually Indonesian slave) birth' (*Stranger Shores*, pp. 308–9). However, the term was in practice much more capacious, coming to refer to a genetically heterogeneous community not only including those typically defined as mixed race: it encompassed autochthonous peoples, slaves from various sites around the Indian Ocean rim (Indonesia, but also Madagascar, and parts of southern

India and mainland south-east Asia), and also 'black' people who had adopted English or white Afrikaans names, or so-called 'Europeans' who chose to identify with mixed-race or ethnically 'indigenous' groups. The term has been problematic and contested throughout its history: it was eclipsed in some quarters, during the struggle against Apartheid, by the use of 'black' as a more inclusive term for anyone rendered racially other by 'white' South Africa; it is sometimes rendered in Afrikaans – the first language of a majority of coloured people – simply as *bruin* (brown); and sometimes it has been prefaced by 'so-called'. Coetzee explains, in an essay review of a memoir by fellow South African writer Breyten Breytenbach, that 'with a *C* the term still carries apartheid echoes; with a *c* it is more or less neutral' (*Stranger Shores*, p. 308). Critic Zoë Wicomb concurs (1998, pp. 93–4), and I use this form here unless referring specifically to Apartheid-era classification. It is still in widespread use as a term of self-identification, particularly in the province of the Western Cape, where coloured South Africans form a majority of the population (see Adhikari).

Lurie's engagement of coloured prostitutes suggests that Farodia Rassool (who I have suggested is also almost certainly meant to be read as coloured, and probably Malay) is correct to sketch a continuum between his sexual behaviour and a longer 'history of exploitation' in South Africa (p. 53). Significantly, when the arrangement with the first Soraya ceases, the escort agency offers Lurie another '[e]xotic' woman (p. 7): they offer him a choice of 'Malaysian, Thai, Chinese' (p. 8), raising the spectre of the exploitation of trafficked women, and of sex-tourism to Asia, too, in addition to the history of slaves from south-east Asia in colonial-era South Africa. Melanie, interestingly, is described – through David's focalization – as having 'almost Chinese cheekbones' (p. 11), and wearing 'baubles from the Oriental Plaza' (p. 37), associating her with the other 'exotic' women in David's life (and in his pay). But it is her name, and David's manipulation of it, that marks Melanie as almost definitely coloured: he thinks of her as 'Meláni', meaning 'the dark one' (p. 18, see p. 78), and 'Melanie-Meláni' (p. 37). In *Sunset at the Globe Salon*, she plays a coloured stereotype, with a 'glaringly *Kaaps*' accent (p. 24, see glossary). Melatonin is, of course, the pigment associated with skin colour; ironically, Lucy's child will be mixed race, will be (crudely) melanized.

While these ethnic or racial markers sometimes escape the non-South African reader, most readers are likely to conclude that Lucy's rapists are 'black'. David tells Lucy that he does not think that she would speak of them as she does if they 'had been white thugs' (p. 159). His statement has two resonances: she feels complicit in white oppression in the past and is thus willing to think that such violence is repayment (he suggests), and that she would not speak of them with such hatred were they white – 'I am not blaming you', he says (p. 159). David's indignation, and empathy, here, indicates the nub of the problem identified in the ANC response to the novel, to which I will turn in the chapter on the novel's reception. Some felt that Coetzee was repeating a colonial trope pervasive in 'black peril' narratives of the early twentieth century, which played on fears of black men raping white women (think, too, of *A Passage to India* and of Faulkner's *Light in August*; this trope is by no means specific to South Africa, and recurs in moments of socio-political or economic uncertainty).

Conservative white South African politicians continued to exploit this fear: election posters for the National Party in 1999, the year *Disgrace* appeared, played explicitly on the supposed threat of widespread black rape. *Disgrace*'s representation of black rapists is unquestionably, perhaps inherently, controversial, but Coetzee is well aware of the dangers of representing inter-racial rape. In a 1991 afterword to a reprint of South African-born novelist Daphne Rooke's *Mittee*, Coetzee describes rape as 'the *ne plus ultra* of colonial horror-fantasies', in other words the act than which there is nothing worse (*Stranger Shores*, p. 259). In his 1999 review of Breytenbach's memoir, *Dog Heart* (intriguingly also engaging with representations of violence, and dogs, here as metaphor), Coetzee voiced disquiet about the way stories of black-on-white violence, particularly in the countryside, played into racist stereotypes (an expanded version of the review appears in *Stranger Shores*, pp. 304–17).

What, then, might we say in Coetzee's defence? He does not flinch from representing (or referring to, remembering that the rape occurs, effectively, off-stage) an act that could not be said, alas, to be unlikely or unusual in South Africa. A writer who refused to write according to the terms dictated by the Apartheid regime, neither was Coetzee going to bow to concerns about political correctness in the new democratic dispensation. The serious writer's task is, after all, if not to bear witness, then to challenge readers' received opinions. But the reader should notice that there are few overt indications of race in the narration of the attack. The attackers, 'two men and a boy', walk (in David's opinion) 'with countrymen's long strides' (p. 91); the majority of rural South Africans are black, but this description, bearing the mark of Lurie's romanticizing of the pastoral (to which we will return) offers no overt description of race. When Lucy shouts at the men taunting the dogs, she does so in Xhosa (*'Hamba!'*), the first language of the majority black population of the Eastern Cape (about which more later), and the syntax of the assailant who explains why they want to use the telephone – 'His sister ... is having an accident' – also suggests a second-language English (and specifically a first-language black Xhosa-language) speaker (p. 92).

The label 'black' is, however, not applied expressly to the attackers during the episode. Rather, the reference is oblique: David 'blacks out' (p. 93) after being attacked. Later the German neighbour, Ettinger, 'remarks darkly' about Petrus (p. 109). Both instances draw attention to how blackness and darkness figure negatively in colloquial speech and popular discourse, and challenge the reader not to draw conclusions about the attackers based solely on race. The first direct application of 'black' to people is only indirectly linked to the attackers: Lurie, looking at the bared teeth of one of the dogs shot dead in the attack, thinks about South Africa being 'a country where dogs are bred to snarl at the mere smell of a black man' (p. 110), implying of course that this dog had done just this before its death.

It is in relation to Petrus that the most overt language of race is deployed by Lurie. He is incensed at Petrus for protecting one of the attackers, and when Bev Shaw defends Petrus, Lurie accuses her of thinking that 'Petrus is an old-style kaffir' just because he 'has a beard and smokes a pipe and carries a stick' (p. 140). Lurie's use of the word 'kaffir', a racist epithet for black South African, is inflammatory and highly offensive, although here he appears to think he is disabusing Bev of what he construes as old-fashioned, liberal-paternalistic attitudes towards rural Africans. It says a great deal more about Lurie's own discomfort with the changes in post-Apartheid South Africa, however. 'In the old days one could have had it out with Petrus', he thinks earlier in relation to Petrus's absence from the farm during the attack (p. 116), but Petrus is no longer the black man for hire, the 'boy' he would have been labelled, pejoratively and dismissively (p. 152) in 'the old days' (Ettinger, significantly, still uses it thus [p. 109]). Rather, Petrus is Lucy's 'co-proprietor' (p. 62) and 'neighbour' (p. 117). David Attwell suggests that we might read Coetzee's use of Petrus to refer to Peter, etymologically a rock and the founder of a new dispensation (2002, p. 335). Petrus is, in this reading, a harbinger of the new dispensation.

Names are often suggestive or symbolic in Coetzee's fiction: Lucy derives from the Latin *lux* and signifies light, Melanie darkness. Lucy or Lucia is also a Catholic patron saint of the blind, and of writers; the metaphoric resonances are clear in her role as a guide to her father, countering his repeated apologies for being a weak guide himself (pp. 79, 156). David's surname is rendered as 'Lourie' in news reports (pp. 115–16), and he subsequently assumes this version (p. 211): *loeries* are South African birds, an apt link for a character interested in song, and the word also suggests *alluring, luring* and, indeed, *lurid*. A real-life David Lurie is also a noted Cape Town-born and London-resident documentary photographer, active from the early 1990s (and who once taught in the Philosophy department at the University of Cape Town). Lurie might also be a Scottish or Irish surname – but I want here to comment on the largely unremarked-upon possibility that Coetzee wants the reader to intuit that Lurie may be Jewish, because Lurie is also a version of the eastern Ashkenazy family name 'Loria' or 'Luria', a family genealogists trace back to the Israelite King David (see Rosenstein), which includes links to families like Isserles and Mendelssohn that have appropriately musical connections for Coetzee's purposes. Lurie's first name might also be said, in this context, to draw on associations with the Biblical David – a musician, and also a man not averse to pursuing only apparently unattainable women.

Lucy Graham (2002) suggests that Lurie's 'Jewish patronym' links him 'as a cipher, to an "Abrahamic tradition"' (p. 7), using this suggestion to develop an argument that Melanie's surname, Isaacs, names her as a loved one marked for sacrifice – an allusion to the Judaeo-Christian narrative of Abraham, who was called upon to sacrifice his son Isaac, for whom his God substituted a ram at the last moment (David, of course, identifies with Petrus's sheep). Coetzee clearly intends readers to think about sacrifice in relation to Melanie – and Soraya: Lurie gives her a present at Eid (p. 5), the Islamic festival associated with Abraham's attempted sacrifice (in the Islamic tradition, it is of his son Ishmael). But how convincing is the suggestion that Lurie may be Jewish? He has 'olive skin' (p. 7), although this is inconclusive (and problematic: once more, Coetzee invites a reading of racial markers while frustrating attempts to determine race categorically). There are, however, four significant moments that deserve further scrutiny. Two are from Petrus's land-grant celebration, during which Petrus uses a gesture – rubbing thumb and forefinger together to signify expense and parsimoniousness – that Lurie recognizes as one '[u]sed of Jews, in the old days'. While he speculates that Petrus's use is likely coincidental, that he is 'innocent of that snippet of European tradition' (p. 130), David's identification of the gesture suggests sensitivity towards anti-Semitism. His possible Jewish identity is suggested more strongly when, on returning to the party after accompanying Lucy back to the house, he feels himself an outsider, and then places his hand on the white skullcap he wears to protect his wounds, claiming it as a sign of his status: 'For the first time he is glad to have it, to wear it as his own' (p. 135). This gesture might well be read as suggesting the acceptance of a previously disavowed identity – a skullcap, or yarmulke, is, of course, worn by men in the Jewish tradition.

Two other references seem germane, although less definitive: in the final chapter, thinking about what it might mean to be a grandfather, David thinks of this as a 'Joseph' (p. 217), presumably to Lucy constructed as Mary (this is therefore a Christian allusion, although the Biblical Joseph was, of course, Jewish). And David's allusion (in his imaginative reconstruction of Melanie signing the complaint against him) to Zola's famous open letter of 1898, '*J'accuse*' (p. 40), accusing the President of France of anti-Semitism in the prosecution of Alfred Dreyfus, carries, in retrospect, a charged sense of David's association of victimhood and his status as an outsider. Whether or not these suggestions of Lurie's Jewish identity are significant is for the reader to decide. It may be worth noting, however, what Coetzee had to say about a victimized character and sublimated Jewish identity elsewhere. Writing about Kafka in the *New York Review of Books* in 1998 (in an essay that was, tangentially, a review of Mark Harman's new translation of *The Castle*), Coetzee remarks on Max Brod's reading of K. in *The Castle* as (in Coetzee's paraphrase and commentary) a 'new Faust' who does not desire 'ultimate knowledge', but rather a 'minimal grace' consisting of 'the most basic prerequisites of life', 'permission to settle down, to cease to be an outsider' (*Stranger Shores*, p. 94). *Disgrace* draws heavily on the Faust story, of course, and this interpretation of K. might be said to fit David uncannily well, too. Crucially, though, Coetzee suggests that Brod's reading is simplistic: it casts K. as a figure with 'religious meaning' (p. 94), an interpretation Coetzee speculates was influenced by Brod's own Zionism. He applauds Harman for trying to 'rescue Kafka from Brod's version of him'; this was likewise as a conservative, and spiritually directed character (p. 95). Lurie, if in fact Jewish, is rescued from such an over-determined reading: he is an outcast like K., at the mercy of a bureaucracy he does not comprehend, without recourse to 'religious meaning'. Jewish markers might then serve most effectively to indicate David's distance from yet another cultural framework, but also a dimly perceived spiritual longing – he thinks in the opening chapter about 'the overlarge and rather empty human soul' (p. 4), after all – and a sense of being an 'outsider' strongly associated with the condition of exile in the Jewish diaspora.

Setting

The novel hints in various ways that its temporal setting is the second half of 1997. Lurie is 52 (pp. 1, 44) and, after reading the report on the scandal in the *Argus* newspaper (a large-circulation Cape Town daily), he thinks of his own date of birth, 1945. The *Argus* reports his age as 53 (p. 46), but newspaper reports in the novel are clearly not to be trusted: the *Herald* later misspells his surname as 'Lourie' (p. 115). If Lucy's child is due at the end of May (p. 198), the rape is likely to have taken place at the end of August or beginning of September – which fits with Lurie's observation about 'cold winter mornings ... in the uplands of the Eastern Cape' soon after his arrival on the smallholding (p. 68). Although it is unclear exactly how long Lurie spends in Cape Town after his hearing or in Salem before the attack (although he suggests a mere two weeks separates his class on Wordsworth and helping Lucy at the market in Grahamstown [p. 71]), we can surmise that the novel opens around mid-year (fitting with the rainy weather typical of the southern-hemisphere winter in the city [pp. 19–20, 41]), and that his departure from Cape Town takes place sometime in August (he tells Rosalind that '[t]erm is nearly over' [p. 43]; South African universities tend to operate on a system of four quarters, the third running from mid-July to late August). Towards the end of the novel, there is a reference to 'holidaymakers' (p. 191) in the audience at the Dock Theatre, suggesting the South African school summer holidays, which begin in early December. December also includes St Lucy's Day in the Catholic calendar, and is thus a symbolically appropriate time for David to return to Lucy's farm in the Eastern Cape.

These temporal markers might be unexceptional were it not that they signal the narrative beginning around the time the hearings of the Human Rights Violations committee of the Truth and Reconciliation Commission (TRC) concluded (special victims hearings continued until August 1998, and amnesty hearings until 2001). The TRC is a key context for *Disgrace*, as I will make clearer in the section on 'confession' to follow. Established under the terms of the Promotion of National Unity and Reconciliation Act (No 34 of 1995), passed by the newly elected South African Parliament, the TRC was concerned with uncovering, recording, where possible recommending restitution, and where certain conditions were met granting amnesty for gross human rights violations committed during the last decades of the Apartheid era. This provides the context for the staging of Lurie's disciplinary hearing, and suggests too that the novel is concerned with teasing out some of the difficult implications – and failings – of the broader national process of accounting for the past.

Some of the novel's geographical settings require little elucidation: Cape Town, the legislative capital of the Cape Colony, the Union of South Africa, and subsequently of both the white-ruled and the democratic South Africa(s), is the oldest European settlement in the country and, of the major South African cities, most architecturally resonant of the European provenance of its first white planners (it was built, we should not forget, by slaves and hired black and coloured labour). The city of George began as a Dutch East India company forestry outpost in 1776, before being established as a town, named for Britain's then monarch George III, in 1811. David's assertion to Lucy – in the Eastern Cape – that Melanie is 'from this part of the world. From George' (p. 68) is not

strictly true: George is slightly closer to Cape Town than to Grahamstown (and at least five hours' drive from Salem). David's error
suggests, perhaps, his sense that everything outside Cape Town is
homogeneously other. His naming of the Grahamstown-Salem area
(known locally as Lower Albany) as 'old Kaffraria' (p. 122) is also,
strictly, incorrect: Kaffraria was further east, as Kai Easton notes
(p. 119). In a 1993 essay, Coetzee took a local historian to task for
appearing to share 'a tendency, not uncommon' for Capetonians; to
regard the city and its immediate environs 'as both geographically
and ideologically set apart from the passions and cruelties of a
wider South Africa' (*Stranger Shores*, p. 341). The point of these
errors on David's part, then, is to suggest a discomfort with extra-
metropolitan Cape Town or with rural South Africa in general. The
rural Eastern Cape serves more particularly as a frontier zone: it is
his 'darkest Africa' (p. 121).

The 1993 essay from which I have just quoted is a review of
historian Noël Mostert's *Frontiers*, a history of the Eastern Cape –
chiefly in the nineteenth century, during which nine wars were
fought between Britain and the Xhosa people (the amaXhosa) over
the question of land. As Gareth Cornwell points out, the region
thus 'presents itself as the most logical setting for a story concerned at its core with entitlement to the land in post-Apartheid
South Africa' (p. 43), which is certainly one way of reading the
novel. Grahamstown – approximately 550 miles (890 km) from
Cape Town – was established as a garrison settlement in the
second decade of the nineteenth century, but became a significant
town after 1820, when 4,000 British colonists were settled along
the Cape Colony's eastern frontier just east of the town, in effect
to provide a human buffer against the uncolonized regions to the
east ruled by a series of Xhosa chieftaincies. David is, of course,
reading Byron's 1820 letters about his affair with Teresa Guiccioli

(p. 87), establishing a direct link with this seminal date in regional history. Grahamstown grew in size and soon rivalled Cape Town as chief municipality of the colony – in the 1840s, in fact, the colonial parliament held sittings there for several years. Coetzee's review of Mostert's *Frontiers* notes that colonial-era Grahamstown was known for its white inhabitants' extreme racial hatred: there was a real fear of annihilation at the hands of Xhosa warriors until the late 1850s. Today, in Coetzee's words, the town is 'no more than a provincial town' (though also an educational centre; David thinks of getting a job at Rhodes University) and yet 'remains the cradle of British culture in South Africa' and an embodiment of a perceived 'link between white English-speaking South Africans and the liberal traditions (real or imagined) of their land of ancestry' (*Stranger Shores*, pp. 336–7). It seems fitting that these traditions are tested so thoroughly in the novel.

Coetzee concurs with Mostert's view that colonial-era racism amongst white settlers – and their descendants – in the Eastern Cape was predicated on a desire to protect property that was seen as 'social capital'; many settlers were poor, and were looking to advance socially as it had been impossible for them to do in Britain. Consequently, any 'loss of their possessions was felt as a crippling assault upon their social identity', and 'hence, ultimately, the hostility between white and black that characterises the Eastern Cape down to the present day', Coetzee suggests (*Stranger Shores*, p. 337). This contextualizes the particular fear with which David apprehends the possibility of a new system of property circulation, and thinks about history repeating itself, about a 'history of wrong' (p. 156) revisiting latter-day settlers. In the context of the novel's setting in the Eastern Cape, then, David's characterization of his daughter as a 'sturdy young settler' (p. 61) and a 'frontier farmer' (p. 62) has added resonance.

Coetzee's choice of the settler surname Shaw is also suggestive. William Shaw (Bill Shaw's namesake), born in Glasgow in 1798, arrived with the 1820 settlers and served as Methodist minister in Salem – he in fact suggested the town's name (Cornwell, p. 44). He lived in Grahamstown from 1829 until his departure for Britain in 1856 (he died there in 1872). Shaw established numerous missions among the Xhosa, becoming Superintendent of the Wesleyan Missions in the region. The frontier was thus both a site of violent conflict over land, but also of acculturation: missionaries like Shaw were guided by an evangelical zeal, but also a 'humanitarian philanthropism', in Coetzee's words (*Stranger Shores*, p. 333), which seems an antecedent of the concern with community and friendship displayed by Bill Shaw (see p. 102). Bev's zeal for animal welfare significantly also makes David think of 'Christians of a certain kind': they are both, he implies, so 'cheerful and well-intentioned that after a while you itch to go off and do some raping and pillaging' (p. 73). Bev ministers to animals, a new constituency for concern under a dispensation that takes little heed of them (they come 'nowhere' '[o]n the list of the nation's priorities', Lucy tells David on p. 73), but also, in her own way, to Lucy and to David. We might recall that David, in a moment of crisis, also thinks himself like 'a missionary' at one point, as if in a grotesque and politically incorrect cartoon, about to be boiled alive by cannibalistic 'savages' (p. 95).

Gerald Gaylard notes that Salem derives from 'shalom' and 'salaam', Hebrew and Arabic for *peace*, and is also part of Jeru*salem* (p. 324). Its choice as a setting might thus suggest the hopefulness with which Lucy attempts to be a new kind of settler (negotiating what might be termed a local solution, and refusing the term 'farm' [p. 200] as too loaded with the baggage of settler and colonial history). In fact, the historical Salem – as Gareth Cornwell discusses usefully (pp. 44–6) – was the site of an early rapprochement between the 1820 settlers and local Xhosa pastoralists. A famous episode in which Richard Gush (1789–1858), a devout Quaker from Devon, who was a settler in 1820, negotiated a peace with a Xhosa group, was the subject of a play by Grahamstown-based writer and academic Guy Butler, performed in 1970 to celebrate the 150th anniversary of the settlers' arrival (published in 1982, and filmed in 1984). It is also surely suggestive that Lucy and Helen had initially lived in Salem as part of a commune, an association of idealistic young people with an unorthodox view of property relations. Salem, however, has other connotations, too: in an American context, it suggests witch trials, gender violence, and oppressive orthodoxies. It may also be telling that Lucy's commune split up with members relocating to 'New Bethesda' (strictly Nieu Bethesda) in the Karoo. The New Testament Bethesda (in the Gospel of John) was a pool in Jerusalem, and as Bethesda derives from the Aramaic *beth hesda*, place or house of mercy, their departure suggests that Salem was no longer a utopia – it may rather be a place without mercy, without grace.

Romanticism

When, towards the end of the novel, Petrus appears to offer to marry Lucy, Lurie stops himself protesting that this would not be how '*We Westerners*' would behave (p. 202). Lurie regards Western – specifically European – models of culture and behaviour as preeminent markers of civility: his familiarity with 'Western' literature, philosophy, music, art, dance and drama attests overwhelmingly to this. On the first page he alludes to Baudelaire, and goes on in Chapter 1 to refer to Greek tragedy (*Oedipus* [p. 2]), Christian Church history (St Benedict [p. 2], Origen [p. 9]), Verdi's opera *Rigoletto* (in the phrase *la donna è mobile* [p. 3]), Byron

(p. 4) and Flaubert's *Madame Bovary* (pp. 5–6). Each of these references shores up Lurie's self-justificatory thoughts about desire, and his own 'temperament'. Readers also learn in this chapter (on p. 4) about Lurie's three scholarly books – on the legend of Faust, the works of Richard of St Victor and English Romantic poet William Wordsworth. Not only are these interests European, but they also suggest Lurie's scholarly engagement with questions of individual identity. All also suggest the risks of overreaching, over-contemplation, and solipsism: Faust strikes a bargain with the devil, Richard of St Victor was an 'ascetic Scots contemplative in a medieval French monastery' (B. McDonald 2009, p. 65), and Wordsworth's concern with introspection and the growth of individual consciousness is one of the strongest in the Romantic movement (a pan-European movement, with its height in different countries in slightly different periods, from the late 1790s to the 1850s).

Each of Lurie's Western intellectual and emotional touchstones – numerous others are alluded to throughout the novel (and some glossed in the glossary in Chapter 5 of this guide) – are tested in the Eastern Cape. Like Faust (and Lucifer), Lurie falls (metaphorically); his identification with Wordsworth is put under strain by very different versions of the pastoral; and, after the attack, even '[t]he word *vision*' appears 'suddenly too old-fashioned, too queer' (p. 103). Locked in Lucy's lavatory, Lurie muses that his knowledge of European languages will not be able to 'save him here in darkest Africa' (p. 95). Later he wonders whether English is a fit language for communication in the country (p. 117); it seems 'tired' (p. 129) and on the verge of collapse. In the context of his perception of the inadequacy of European cultural referents – and languages – in South Africa, the title of the play *Sunset at the Globe Salon* itself offers ironically symbolic commentary on Lurie's identifications: the Globe was Shakespeare's theatre, and a *salon* a very Enlightenment European venue for cultured exchange. *Sunset* suggests that both, or what both might be said to represent, are on the wane.

Lurie's interest in Romanticism is particularly significant. As Graham Pechey points out, colonization on the Eastern frontier coincided with a brand of English Romanticism allied with a counter-Enlightenment spirit that cast 'poetry as the vehicle of struggle against a reason seen as oppressive' (p. 380), and proposed that the real truths of human experience could not be governed entirely by reason – hence the antipathy of Romantic poet, artist, and visionary, William Blake, towards Isaac Newton, the great representative for him of the narrowness of Enlightenment science ('May God us keep / From Single vision and Newton's sleep!', he declared in 1802 [Blake, p. 818]). At the beginning of *Disgrace*, Lurie would in all likelihood endorse Blake's aphoristic statements in 'There is No Natural Religion' (c. 1788) that 'Man cannot naturally Perceive but through his natural or bodily organs' (Blake, p. 97). This might have served in place of the aphorism Lurie quotes from Blake's *The Marriage of Heaven and Hell* (c. 1790–3) in justifying to Lucy his commitment to acting according to desire (p. 69).

For Wordsworth, this counter-Enlightenment spirit took the form of a pantheistic idea of a life-force in all things, and an insistence on the ethical imperative of sympathetic imagination in – and with – nature. This informs much of Wordsworth's poetry, and particularly the multi-part work *The Prelude*, intended as pre-fatory to a larger project, *The Recluse* (planned with his friend Samuel Taylor Coleridge but which never materialized), and left unfinished in 14 books on his death in 1850. In *Disgrace*, *The Prelude* is a touchstone for David Lurie: he remembers no time in which its 'harmonies' have not 'echoed within him' (p. 13). In Chapter 3, he discusses part of Book Six of *The Prelude* (lines 524–8 of the 1850 text, see Wordsworth, p. 235), a section describing how the image of Mont Blanc falls short of the anticipation of a group of travellers crossing the Alps. The passage suggests that experience is never equal to the imagined ideal. Lurie directs his students to line 599, and offers further discussion: here he is concerned with Wordsworth's attempt to sustain a balance between anticipation and experience, between what Lurie paraphrases as 'pure idea' and 'matter-of-fact clarity' (p. 22), a balance pursued as a means of retaining a sense of the ideal, before its destruction, in order to animate the imagination. Lines 598–602 of *The Prelude* (1850 text) read:

> ... to my conscious soul I now can say –
> 'I recognize thy glory': in such strength
> Of usurpation, when the light of sense
> Goes out, but with a flash that has revealed
> The invisible world, doth greatness make abode[.]
>
> (Wordsworth, p. 239)

Lurie encourages his students to think about the sequence by imagining South African mountains like the Drakensberg range in KwaZulu-Natal, or Table Mountain, which looms above Cape Town. But he senses that he alone continues to see the suggestiveness of his Romantic masters. On another level, he also knows that his reading of this passage is self-interested, that it is linked with his own justification for pursuing Melanie. His disquisition on Wordsworth's attempt to balance the ideal and experience calls to his mind, after all, a memory of first exposing Melanie's breasts (p. 23): the feminine and the landscape become elided in this description, which betrays an acquisitive (heterosexual) male sense of entitlement to experiences of the sublime. Ironically, Wordsworth's famously enigmatic Lucy poems suggest Wordsworthian resonances quite different from these: female experience at one with nature, but in a manner either apparently opaque or lost to the male speaker (see Wu, pp. 326–9, 356–7).

Another key Romantic figure for Lurie is, as we have seen, George Gordon Byron, the Sixth Baron Byron (1788–1824). Lurie plans a chamber opera based on Byron's affair with Teresa Guiccioli, and conducts a class on sections of Byron's long poem *Lara* (1814) in Chapter 4 of *Disgrace* – the quotations in the novel are from Stanza 18 (pp. 32–3; Byron, p. 251). Lurie tells Melanie that many English people like Byron travelled to Italy in the Romantic period, believing 'the Italians were still in touch with their natures' (p. 15). In the context of the novel's opening chapters, in which Lurie thinks much of 'temperament' and is concerned with unrestrained pursuit of his sexual desires, Byron's anti-heroes offer an apt model. As Jerome McGann notes in his edition of Byron, these Byronic (anti-)heroes symbolize 'an experience of psychic and social despair', oppose instituted authority, and form attachments to idealized women (p. 1036). I discussed Lurie's identification with one such hero, Lucifer (in *Lara*), earlier. Like Lucifer, Lurie will fall (metaphorically and literally), and be engulfed by flames.

Before the attack on the smallholding, while at the market in Grahamstown, the smell of burning meat prompts Lurie to muse on the verbs '*burned ... burnt*', recalling his interest during his Romanticism classes in Cape Town a fortnight earlier in the 'perfective' – that which marks aspect in the perfect tense, or, as Lurie explains, signals 'action carried through to its conclusion' (p. 71). The irony of Lurie's concern there with the forms of the verb *usurp* (p. 21), particularly in the context of his probable rape of

Melanie, becomes clearer when, in retrospect, his concern with being burned (or burnt) might be seen to foreshadow his own assault: after it, '[e]verything is tender, everything is burned ... burnt' (p. 97). Lurie thinks, too, about this verb when he visits Melanie's father and tells him that she sparked a 'fire' in him (p. 166). Lurie's class on Wordsworth also dwelt on the idea of the sense image 'burned on the retina' (p. 22). Cumulatively, the linking of Romanticism with this interest in the perfective serves to signal Lurie's entrapment: the perfective indicates past action, although action recently past (the consequences of which continue), and the novel's third-person present-tense narration renders Lurie's obsession with the verb form ironic – for him, disgrace is an indefinite sentence (p. 172). Lurie, Gerald Gaylard argues, is 'unable to live up to his own Wordsworthian ideal of a balance between archetype and reality' – or, we might add, to his sense of the pathos of the Byronic anti-hero's devotion to desire – 'because he is rapt in his own ecstasy' (p. 320). He remains trapped in identifications with European archetypes and visions increasingly out of place in his changing environment.

Form

Several references have already been made to the novel's use of limited third-person present-tense narration – what DelConte calls 'heterodiegetic simultaneous present tense narration' (p. 443) – and its focalization through David Lurie. This section does not offer a detailed stylistic analysis of the novel's form, nor of aspect and voice, issues alluded to sufficiently (and which can be pursued by readers in work by Pechey, Sanders and Wicomb [2002], as well as Spivak, who advances a contentious argument about possible counter-focalization in relation to Lucy). It remains to reiterate that *Disgrace* should be considered as only ostensibly a realist novel: Coetzee, having absorbed the implications of post-structuralism for thinking about language and representation, and having wrestled with the possibilities for writing in periods of historical emergency, produces fiction that is highly conscious of the complicities of any narrative form. The playfully postmodern runs the risk of relativism. Realism runs the risk of hiding its artifice, which can have unintended consequences – for example readers reading *Disgrace* simply as a report on post-Apartheid South Africa. Coetzee himself prefers to call realism 'illusionism', observing in *Doubling the Point* that '[t]he most accomplished illusionism yields the most convincing realist effects' (p. 27).

Coetzee's illusionism is partly indicated by *Disgrace*'s generic instability: the narrative tries out a number of genres in order to tell David Lurie's story – or, rather, the story *of* David Lurie, as seen through his eyes. David's focalization suggests stubborn self-justification: he will not perform contrition; he justifies his dedication to act according to his desire. Later, he offers his own kind of confession when he apologizes to Lucy for being unable to save her – 'That is his own confession' (p. 157). And if *Disgrace* is an academic or campus novel in its first half, it moves into the mode of the pastoral (perhaps more strictly the *anti*-pastoral) in the second, although by turns this is further inflected as idyllic, tragic or comic (for example, David's synoptic narrative to the Isaacs family over dinner seems to him to be a story of rural life 'in all its idiot simplicity' [p. 170]). At moments, David's own self-narrativization appears to share the pretensions of his planned opera, but then, as the context changes, it 'sounds melodramatic' (p. 66) and slips into a very different register. The final section of this chapter now considers two issues relevant to this code-switching, but also to the novel's serious investigation of the forms pertinent to contemporary, post-Apartheid South Africa, to narratives of trauma, alterity, gender violence and dispossession more broadly. These, framed here as 'forms' while just as much themes and contexts, are the pastoral, and confession.

Pastoral

In an interview in *Doubling the Point*, Coetzee muses on the nature of the pastoral, suggesting that 'the idea of the local solution' is at its centre; it 'defines and isolates a space in which whatever cannot be achieved in the wider world (particularly the city) can be achieved' (p. 61), he suggests. This offers an intriguing way of viewing as a kind of local solution Lucy's decision to remain in Salem and reach an accommodation with Petrus that seems – at least to her – appropriate to post-Apartheid circumstances. David finds it strange that he and Evelina (a name surely symbolic of Eve), both 'cityfolk', could have produced such a 'sturdy young settler' (p. 61), but his use of this loaded term in the context of the Eastern Cape indicates his outmoded thinking. Lucy, obviously more attuned to the costs of such acquisitive concepts, refuses to have her smallholding called a 'farm': 'it's just a piece of land where I grow things' (p. 200), she insists. Her attempt at a new relationship with the land seems to be symbolized by her walking barefoot on the soil, something David notes about her immediately upon his arrival on the smallholding (pp. 59, 62).

The distance between David's outdated sense of the pastoral and the reality of rural South Africa soon becomes clear, even to him. He is initially charmed by '[c]ountry ways' (p. 65) – for example, the manners of local schoolchildren – but soon realizes that the countryside is not the idyll he imagined (see p. 125, and Barnard 2002). In the first chapter, noting that he is 'a man of the city' (p. 6), he speculates that the 'hum of traffic' that he finds soothing might have its parallel for 'countryfolk' in the appeal of silence (p. 5). However, on his first night in Lucy's house, he finds country nights far from silent: he is woken by barking dogs (p. 67). Later, he finds the pace of life in the country boring (p. 76). By the final chapter, as he watches Lucy in her garden and thinks it a 'scene ready-made for a Sargent or a Bonnard', he admits that this aesthetic rendering is out of touch with reality: those artists were '[c]ity boys like him', he admits, conceding that 'despite all his reading in Wordsworth', 'he has never had much of an eye for rural life ...' (p. 218).

Coetzee writes insightfully about the pastoral mode in the culture of white South African literature in his 1988 book, *White Writing*. There he holds to account different European responses to Africa, including the Afrikaans-language genre of the farm novel, the *plaasroman*, which is concerned with ownership of the land, and the investment of a sense of identity in the land (we might recall the young John's feelings about his father's family's farm, in *Boyhood*, esp. pp. 79–97), and another mode in which Africa is a vast, empty space, apparently existing outside of time. Rita Barnard (2007) calls these two 'mythic maps' respectively 'arcadian' and 'dystopian' (p. 28). Crucially, in the South African context, both involved obscuring the long presence of black South Africans in the landscape, and their continued labour in it, Coetzee explains in *White Writing* (see p. 5). In *Boyhood*, both approaches inform the young John's responses to his father's family's farm: he has a complicated relationship of belonging to it (*'I belong to the farm'*), but also senses that it is a space that refuses ownership: it 'belongs to no one' and 'exists from eternity to eternity' (1998, p. 96). He recognizes, too, that if anyone *had* a claim to it, it would not be the whites who presume to own it. Of rural coloured people, John thinks: 'Not only do they come with the land, the land comes with them, is theirs, has always been' (*Boyhood* [1998], p. 62).

In an address delivered on receiving the Jerusalem Prize (in 1987), Coetzee suggested that a white South African investment in the land involved a failure to recognize the aspirations of all of its human inhabitants. 'At the heart of the unfreedom of the hereditary masters of South Africa', he argued, 'is a failure of love', and continued as follows:

> To be blunt: their love is not enough today and has not been enough since they arrived on the continent; furthermore, their talk, their excessive talk, about how they love South Africa has consistently been directed toward *the land*, that is, toward what is least likely to respond to love: mountains and deserts, birds and animals and flowers.
>
> (*DP*, p. 97)

Lucy's pastoralism involves a return to the status of a peasant working the land, rather than of a hereditary master directing the labour of others. Her partnership with Petrus is crucial in this regard, and it makes of the black labourer a new kind of South African farmer (at least as far as David is concerned), that is a challenge for her father to understand. When Lucy suggests David help Petrus on the smallholding, David retorts that he likes 'the historical piquancy', and wonders whether Petrus will pay him a 'wage' (p. 77). Petrus fits none of the models of (racialized) farm labour to which David has access, and David is surprised at Petrus's enthusiasm and industry – 'swift and businesslike; all very unlike Africa' (p. 151) – in ploughing his land. David uses many European terms for *peasant* in the course of the narrative, including for Petrus (see especially p. 117). Interestingly, Cornwell points out, John Barrow, an early nineteenth-century traveller who wrote about the interior of the Cape, used the term 'African peasant' for specifically *white* frontier farmers (p. 49, see *White Writing*, p. 73). If peasantry is the new mode of pastoralism fit for the new South Africa, effectively a new 'local solution', then Lucy and Petrus share an equal status in the enterprise.

Confession

A significant context for any discussion of confession in South Africa in the late 1990s is the Truth and Reconciliation Commission (TRC), constituted by law and chaired by Nobel Peace Laureate and noted human rights advocate Archbishop Desmond Tutu. It sought, during the middle and late 1990s, to uncover the thousands of stories of human rights abuses committed under the Apartheid regime, and to consider amnesty applications brought by perpetrators. It was a requirement for amnesty that perpetrators give a full and frank account of what they had done, and that they prove a political motive for their actions. Although there was an unspoken expectation that an act of repentance would be performed, perpetrators did not, strictly speaking, have to apologize or prove contrition. Rather, amnesty was construed as necessary for reconciliation, although the TRC's critics would claim in due course that justice was made subordinate to reconciliation in the process (see Sanders, Posel further).

Despite its requirements for a kind of confession that was not delivered in pursuit of absolution or forgiveness endorsed in religious terms, that the TRC was chaired by a cleric gave the whole enterprise a religious air. Notice how the disciplinary hearing in Chapter 6 of *Disgrace* operates in a comparable manner. It is chaired by a Professor of Religious Studies, Manas Mathabane (p. 47). However, David Lurie's response to questioning might be read as an implied critique of the ambiguities attendant on the

TRC's process. He refuses to offer a confession on the terms demanded by the more hostile members of the panel, especially Farodia Rassool (p. 52). She insists that Lurie acknowledge a distinction between pleading guilty to an offence, which he does, and demonstrating contrition, which he refuses to do. He offers a formula: he 'took advantage'; it was 'wrong'; he feels 'regret' (p. 54). When this continues to be insufficient for Rassool, who demands that he prove his sincerity, Lurie objects strenuously that this would be 'beyond the scope of the law' (p. 55).

He effectively resists all attempts to demand confession in a non-secular framework, in which, in his view, it has little meaning: confession is conventionally involved with guilt and the promise of absolution, expiation, and salvation. He notes that the panel is a 'secular tribunal'; he can consequently only be expected to enter a 'secular plea', which bears in no way on the quasi-religious idea of repentance. That, he says, suggests 'another universe of discourse' altogether (p. 58). Lurie is resolutely secular: he tells Mr Isaacs that he is 'not a believer' (p. 172), though he clearly accepts religious discourse as part of the inheritance of Western culture, reflecting negatively on the post-religious sensibilities of his students, for example (p. 32). But he insists on maintaining the logic by which secular society deals with transgression. Elsewhere, he dismisses the usefulness of the metaphor of the scapegoat (or its applicability to his case) because it only functions with the backing of religious sanction (p. 91).

And yet the novel suggests that Lurie's position might ultimately be inadequate – even if, rationally, there seems little alternative for him. In conversation with Mr Isaacs, for example, he seems desperate to discover what it is that might end his state of disgrace. Isaacs asks him to '[b]reak bread' with them (p. 167), invoking religious discourse, and Lurie responds with an inappropriate 'offering' – the Isaacses are teetotal – of wine (p. 168). Later, he does attempt his own gesture of atonement, as if attempting to think himself into this alien discursive order: he prostrates himself awkwardly in front of Melanie's mother and sister (p. 173), apparently enacting bodily an expression of abnegation.

Coetzee has long been concerned with confession in narrative, and with what he calls a condition of grace – which he defines as that which is opposed to cynicism, to 'the denial of any ultimate basis for values' (*DP*, p. 392). In this regard, his 1985 essay 'Confession and Double Thoughts: Tolstoy, Rousseau, Dostoevsky' (included in *Doubling the Point*) is significant. Its most important observation, David Attwell suggests, is 'that truth in confession cannot be arrived at by introspection alone': resolution, or 'release' is possible only 'with an affirmation or imposition of truth – alternatively, from grace. This is not an easy lesson for a secular, critical postmodernism to absorb, but it is one that enables Coetzee to address more directly the crucial problem of narrative authority' (*DP*, p. 11). As this formulation suggests, the nature of confession – the form that it imposes, or demands, particularly in a secular age – is central to the manner in which *Disgrace* deals with David Lurie's predicament. Coetzee himself, in interview, speaks of the 'body with its pain' as 'a counter to the endless trials of doubt': 'Not grace, then, but at least the body' (*DP*, p. 248). What Coetzee seems to mean here is that where once grace might have come from absolution in a religious sense (the end of confession), in a secular age it might rather come in the form of an intervention, an act or presence bestowing or enacting grace. This might take the form of charity: 'charity... is, I suppose, the way in which grace allegorizes itself in the world' (*DP*, p. 249). Or it might take the form of recognition of the suffering body: 'Let me put it baldly',

Coetzee writes in *Doubling the Point*, 'in South Africa it is not possible to deny the authority of suffering and therefore of the body' (p. 248). In Lucy Graham's words (2002), 'Coetzee proposes that the body, with its frailty and suffering, is a counter to the endless scepticism that is a feature of both secular confession and textual analysis' (p. 6). We might read Lurie's prostration before Mrs Isaacs and Desiree as another act of self-interested performance, or as an attempt at bodily abnegation. Similarly, we might (or might not) read the novel's final chapters as forcing his recognition of the suffering body – not only of his daughter, but of animals too.

3

The Novel's Reception

The noted South African playwright Athol Fugard, in a profile published in the London *Sunday Times* in January 2000 (and quickly reprinted in South Africa's *Sunday Independent*), reacted violently to *Disgrace*'s representation of Lucy's speculation that rape might be the price for being able to stay on in post-Apartheid South Africa. That, at least, is how Fugard understood Lucy's conversation with David about the issue, although he had not read the novel: 'I haven't read it, and I'm sure the writing is excellent, ... but I could not think of anything that would depress me more than this book by Coetzee – *Disgrace* – where we've got to accept the rape of a white woman as a gesture to all the evil we did in the past', Fugard said, concluding: 'That's a load of bloody bullshit' (quoted in Marais 2001, p. 32). Many South African reviewers, politicians and writers responded equally negatively to the novel in the first year after its publication – including, famously, as I will discuss towards the end of this chapter, high-ranking members of the country's governing party, the ANC. Coetzee's novel understandably raised hackles in a country with a brutal history, facing enormous challenges in the final years of the millennium; it seemed deliberately, perhaps perversely, to challenge readers not to read it as straightforward realism, a report on conditions in the country, or as an allegory of the 'New' South Africa. Lucy tells David that he is missing the point in thinking that her decision not to report what happened to her is based on 'abstractions' or ideas (p. 112). Some responses to Coetzee's novel might, one imagines, have been greeted by the novelist with a similar response.

By contrast, much of the novel's early reception, particularly in foreign reviews, was extremely positive. Writing in the London *Independent* on 3 July 1999, Paul Bailey called *Disgrace* 'a subtle, multi-layered story', praising Coetzee's style as 'chaste and lyrical without being self-conscious'. Barbara Trapido, a South African-born novelist herself, wrote in the same newspaper the following day that *Disgrace* was 'bleakly beautiful' and managed to say 'something close to the bone about the state of contemporary South Africa'. Eileen Battersby, writing in the *Irish Times* in August, called it 'a work of immense artistry', while Felix Cheong, in a review in the Singaporean paper *The Straits Times*, praised its 'taut, haunting prose': it was 'almost like poetry strung across the page throbbing with elegiac regret', he wrote. Sandra Martin, reviewing the novel in the Canadian *Globe and Mail*, drew attention to its 'elegant and allegorical role reversals', 'spare symbolism' and complex characterization. She noted, too, that readers may not 'like' Lurie, but that this was part of Coetzee's design.

As the novel gained attention globally, and appeared on the Booker Prize shortlist (as I will discuss in Chapter 4), longer reviews began to appear, offering engagements with its contexts – Coetzee's career to that point, as well as recent South African history. The first and amongst the best of these is Elizabeth

Lowry's long review of both *Disgrace* and *The Lives of Animals*, in the *London Review of Books*. Lowry draws careful attention to Coetzee's theoretical sophistication, noting how, in a writing career by then stretching over 25 years, he had drawn frequently on an understanding of postmodern narrative strategies in order to critique the legacies of expansionist European political and philosophical modes of thought. She notes that Coetzee's writing self-consciously raises issues 'of the cultural authority to which fiction written in the Western tradition can lay claim', supporting her suggestion that readers should not engage with *Disgrace* as simply an apparently realistic representation or critique of conditions in post-Apartheid South Africa. Lowry draws readers' attention to the dilemmas that writers from South Africa had long faced, whether to succumb to a deeply felt desire either to represent conditions under Apartheid or to resist the imperatives of the political. *Disgrace*, Lowry concluded, was 'the best novel' that Coetzee had yet produced; it was 'the work of a mature writer who has refined his textual obsessions to produce an exact, effective prose and condensed his thematic concern with authority into a deceptively simple story...'. (In the run of extremely perceptive reviews, Lowry's, and also Attwell's – in the academic *Journal of Southern African Studies*, in December 2001 – are unsurpassed.)

Critics had begun to draw attention to some of the narrative's less obvious characteristics and strategies. Thus, for example, Peter Goldsworthy, writing in the Australian *Sydney Morning Herald* two days before the Booker Prize ceremony in late October, noted that Coetzee never introduces characters 'by race', that readers had 'to guess from context'. Goldsworthy wondered whether this was an element in Coetzee's 'cunning', in other words, whether he meant 'to confront' readers with their 'own expectations, to make us read through the fogged lens of our own assumptions'.

Goldsworthy concluded that *Disgrace* was the 'most morally interesting novel' he had read in years. Michael Gorra, writing in the *New York Times* in late November 1999 (after the novel was awarded the Booker Prize in London on 25 October), commented on the novel's narrative perspective and on Lurie's interest in the perfective, suggesting that 'Coetzee's most impressive achievement' grew 'from the very bones of the novel's grammar'. 'This novel stands as one of the few I know', Gorra concluded, 'in which the writer's use of the present tense is in itself enough to shape the structure and form of the book as a whole'.

In the *Village Voice* in December 1999, Benjamin Kunkel offered a nuanced reading that drew connections between Lurie's disciplinary hearing and the TRC. He also suggested that it was a 'departure' from Coetzee's earlier fondness for allegory: 'Indeed, among the many themes of this diamond of a novel ... is the frustrated temptation of allegory: the desire of sufferers to signify something beyond themselves'. (Maya Jaggi, writing in the British *Guardian* newspaper in November 1999, disagreed; for her, *Disgrace* was indeed allegorical, a 'parable of the New South Africa'.) Kunkel's comment is suggestive: he argues that if we read Coetzee's 1983 novel, *Life & Times of Michael K*, as 'a kind of protest against allegory' (Michael K refuses to be made to signify anything other than his own body), then *Disgrace* could be seen to explore a related but inverted situation. Conditions in a new dispensation meant that people were not made to signify – for example, in terms purely of race – in the way that had been the case during the Apartheid era: 'one of the freedoms of a free society is the freedom not to mean anything, not to suffer official categorization', Kunkel suggested. However, in such circumstances, as 'the individual's rights are restored to him, so is his smallness', Kunkel observed: the individual's 'life does not go beyond itself'. This, he suggests perceptively, may be what David Lurie must discover at the end of the novel.

Some reviewers, like John Banville (in the *New York Review of Books* in January 2000), appeared however not to appreciate all of the novel's complex operations. Banville, an eminent novelist himself, thought Coetzee over-ambitious. The chamber opera, for example, seemed to him to fit 'oddly' into the novel, perhaps having been included merely 'as a counterpoint' to the book's bleakness. He felt that the episodes with Soraya and Melanie were too brief, and these figures insufficiently characterized for Lurie's attraction to Melanie to be plausible, or for Soraya's motivations to be entirely clear. Lucy, too, appeared to him to be vaguely drawn, fading in places 'into a haziness in which she is more symbol than solid human being'. These criticisms appear not to give due regard to the novel's focalization through Lurie. Banville also thought that the descriptions of Lurie's disciplinary hearing were not as 'telling as one suspects the author imagines them to be'; he appeared not to notice possible parallels with the TRC at all.

Some of these critiques were shared, though in many cases made more vigorously, by some of the negative reviews that greeted *Disgrace*. Amongst the earliest of these international responses came in the *Scotsman*, where Michael Pye asserted that the novel showed Coetzee's obsession with disillusion, and left 'a wretched, sour taste'. He felt in particular that the novel's final bleak images were 'patronising to the reader' who had persevered with the narrative. Keith Nickson, writing in *The Toronto Star* at the end of October 1999 (after the Booker Prize had been announced), felt that *Disgrace* was too didactic, its characters' 'reversals in fortunes and inversions of power relationships' improbably 'jarring', and that Coetzee was too wedded to symbolism. James Hynes, writing in the *Washington Post* in January 2000, agreed: 'the book

reads less like a novel and more like a very elegant, very complicated moral dilemma concocted for a graduate seminar in ethics',
he argued. Hynes felt that the parallel drawn between Lurie's
abuse of Melanie and the gang-rape was too obvious, preventing
the book working as fiction. In fact, he argued, *Disgrace* read too
much like a Calvinist sermon: it carried 'the whiff of brimstone'
and, in insisting on what he took to be an 'improving' message,
'refuse[d] finally to accept all the possibilities of fiction'.

Some South African reviewers also felt that aspects of the novel
militated against it being read as fiction: for many, it was what was
seen as pointed commentary on the position of whites in the post-
Apartheid nation that was particularly difficult to dissociate from
the novel's narrative perspective and pointed ironies. Glenn Hollands, writing in the *Daily Dispatch*, a newspaper published in the
Eastern Cape city of East London, warned that the novel would
'leave most readers squirming with discomfort and denial'. The
discomfort was palpable: the Afrikaans writer Dan Roodt shared
this criticism, and drew on the novel in coining the term 'Lucy-
syndrome' to refer to the idea that white South Africans had to be
prepared to accept abasement and abnegation to atone for the
wrongs of the Apartheid era (Marais 2001, p. 32). Critic Michael
Marais countered by arguing that to interpret *Disgrace* as 'merely . . .
a manifestation of "Liberal Funk" or as an articulation of a politics
of white abasement', as many did, was 'to reduce it to a term in
precisely those dualisms that it questions and seeks to destabilize'
(p. 38). Some white critics also, in focusing on Lucy, seemed
prepared to take at his word Lurie's sense that his encounters with
Melanie were not quite rape. Lucy Graham (2003) points out that
several – including Michael Morris in the *Cape Argus*, Toni
Younghusband in the women's magazine *Femina*, and Max du Preez
in the Johannesburg paper *The Star* – described their involvement

as an 'affair'. 'Overlooking the violation entirely, Albert du Toit explains' – in the *Eastern Province Herald*, Graham notes – 'that the "affair" between Lurie and Melanie "blossoms but soon sours"' (p. 440).

If white critics rejected with discomfort what they took as the novel's suggestion about white expectations, black critics objected to the novel's representation of black and coloured characters. Aggrey Klaaste, a veteran journalist long associated with the leading black newspaper *The Sowetan*, objected strongly. He found the depiction of 'black men raping a white woman ... offensive', and berated Coetzee for being overly 'cynical' in giving voice to the kinds of complaints about post-Apartheid South Africa typical (in Klaaste's words) of the 'disgruntled Afrikaner'. Jakes Gerwel, an established academic and civil servant who had run the Office of the President under Nelson Mandela, voiced similar concerns, but this time interestingly in an Afrikaans-language weekly newspaper, *Rapport*. This was perhaps particularly pointed, given Gerwel's status as a leading intellectual – and as a leading coloured intellectual. As Peter McDonald (2002) comments, the review was balanced – it praised Coetzee 'as a compelling chronicler of "the dislocation [*onbehuisdheid*] of the white-in-Africa"' – but barbed. Gerwel objected to what he called (in McDonald's translation) the 'almost barbaric post-colonial claims of black Africans', and also the novel's 'representation of "mixed-race [*bruin*] characters" as "whores, seducers, complainers, conceited accusers", and ... its "exclusion of the possibility of civilized reconciliation"' (p. 325).

The novel was, apparently, discussed by then President Thabo Mbeki's Cabinet, after which – Attwell notes (2004) – 'Coetzee was informally given the dubious ... reassurance that he was "not without his defenders"'. This was not the governing ANC's only engagement with the novel. As both Peter McDonald and Attwell (both 2002) discuss at some length (with differing interpretations), it was cited in a submission made by the ANC to the Human Rights Commission of Inquiry into racism in the media in South Africa, in April 2000, as evidence of persisting racist attitudes among white South Africans. McDonald notes that the submission might be read in part as suggesting that Coetzee accurately reflects racism (but does not endorse it), although other sections suggest that the drafters of the submission did not necessarily draw a distinction between Lurie and Lucy's opinions and speech, and Coetzee's purported intentions or suggestions (p. 324). Attwell suggests that the submission may have been authored by a small sub-group of senior ANC leaders and was not an officially endorsed ANC document. He suggests, rather, that it tried 'to avoid the philistinism of accusing Coetzee of racism' but also tried 'to use him nevertheless as celebrity witness to its prevalence' (p. 334).

A decade on, and criticism of the novel in official circles in South Africa is largely forgotten: Coetzee was made a member of a prestigious state order in 2005, in recognition of his service to literature (and perhaps in an attempt to offer local praise befitting a Nobel Laureate). Among writers and critics abroad, there seems now to be a widespread sense that the novel is among the most significant of the last quarter-century: it regularly features in 'best of' lists. Coetzee's novel has also been a popular success in many countries, selling numbers perhaps unprecedented for a South African novel since Alan Paton's *Cry, the Beloved Country* (published in 1948). Marni Jackson, in a column in the Canadian *Globe and Mail* in November 2000, commented amusingly on the growing tendency for readers to buy prize-winning books, but to avoid reading them: 'It may be that when you come home from work, you use *The Blind Assassin*' – Margaret Atwood's Booker Prize-winning novel – 'as a kind of mini-TV tray while watching a show about sea turtles', she joked. However, she urged, readers should make an effort with *Disgrace* – it 'keeps on finding new readers', she noted, 'arouses argument, and enriches dinner party chitchat with its unflinching moral vision'. Finally, Jackson suggests, it 'helps us see more clearly, and read with renewed faith. ... And like any good novel, it becomes something new the second time around'.

The novel's capacity for reinterpretation, and its sophisticated engagement with a number of issues with which some strands of literary criticism, social and cultural anthropology, and philosophy are routinely concerned, has generated a large body of academic writing. Conference papers, journal articles, and book chapters on any number of aspects of the novel and its apparent concerns abound: the entries included in the bibliography represent merely a sample of the most significant, helpful, or accessible of these, some of which I have cited in the preceding discussion of the novel (in Chapter 2). Some of the best of these engage with the novel's representation of rape, race, or alterity ('otherness'), some in relation to the rest of Coetzee's oeuvre. Latterly, critics from a range of disciplines have considered the novel's – and its author's – concern with animals, and with issues of representing trauma or of bearing witness. Some critics, like Gayatri Spivak, have cited the novel as evidence in the development of arguments about the politics of speaking for others, and about the politics of university teaching.

4

The Novel's Performance and Adaptation

In this chapter, I consider *Disgrace*'s 'performance' in a broad sense – chiefly its status as prize-winning fiction and its adaptation as a feature film (starring John Malkovich as David Lurie). The novel has also been much discussed by scholars and critics in a large number of essays and articles in academic journals. Increasingly, as Coetzee is becoming recognized as one of the most important Anglophone authors of the last quarter century, the level of critical activity is likely to increase: the bibliography includes only a small sample of the most useful academic discussions of *Disgrace*. It is likely, too, that with 2010 marking the author's 70th birthday, it will not be long before a biography appears in print.

Materiality

One aspect of performance, of course, is how the novel has appeared in print for global audiences. In this regard, it is interesting to pay attention to the cover art that the novel's many publishers – for many translations – have chosen. The British edition featured a photograph, by Lucy Harmer, of a lanky, brindle dog in a desolate landscape featuring an item of rusted machinery of indeterminate origin (while apparently photographed in Norwich, England, it does evoke the Eastern Cape). Danish and Spanish translations featured the same photograph, and the Polish edition also opted for an abject-looking dog. Of course, the novel is partly *about* dogs – though their metaphorical resonances ('Like a dog!') are powerfully evoked in the images chosen. Other translations have elected to represent abjection or isolation differently: a Portuguese edition featured a photograph of a child's mouth and eyes visible through a hole in a battered wooden door. Some publishers chose to focus on race: Germany's Fischer Verlag used a curious photograph of a blonde woman with half of her face painted black; the French mass-market paperback (published by Points) sports a stylized black mask-like face, with features traced in white lines. Some publishers focused on the novel's engagement with gender and sexuality: the Serbian translation (*Sramota*) featured on its cover a detail of Gustave Klimt's painting *The Kiss* (1907–8); an edition of the Dutch translation (*In ongenade*) used a photograph of a female figure curled up on a bed; a Russian translation used an illustration of a small middle-aged man in an overcoat staring into the crotch of a large woman. Still other translations invoke the novel's setting – or a stylized version of its rural setting – in emphasizing the pastoral (or isolation): German, Swiss (French), and Italian editions did this. An edition in Greek featured a photograph of a woman playing a cello (choosing, perhaps predictably, to emphasize the novel's engagement with the Byron narrative). The American Viking Penguin paperback has a suitably enigmatic blank, white cover – suggesting, perhaps most honestly, that the novel is very much what readers make of it.

Prizes

Disgrace was awarded the Booker Prize for Fiction in 1999. Established in 1969 and restricted to novels in English by authors from the United Kingdom, Ireland, and countries of the British Commonwealth, the Booker Prize is conventionally regarded as the most prestigious literary award made in Britain, and one of the most significant in the Anglophone world. Coetzee had won the prize in 1983, for *Life & Times of Michael K*, controversially beating Salman Rushdie's *Shame* to the top spot. In 1999, Rushdie's *The Ground Beneath Her Feet*, widely expected to make the prize shortlist, had not – the other shortlisted novels were Indian novelist Anita Desai's *Fasting, Feasting*, English writer Michael Frayn's *Headlong*, English-resident Egyptian novelist Ahdaf Soueif's *The Map of Love*, Irish writer Colm Tóibín's *The Blackwater Lightship*, and first-time Scottish novelist Andrew O'Hagan's *Our Fathers*. Coetzee's award made him the first novelist to win twice, and earned him £21,000 (£20,000 first prize, and £1,000 awarded to each shortlisted author). Frayn's novel had been widely tipped to win the prize, at least in the arts pages of British newspapers, although rumours later circulated that the journalist and writer Natasha Walter, one of the judges, vetoed Frayn's novel as insufficiently serious. *Disgrace* appeared to be the book on which there was least disagreement on the night: the judges reportedly deliberated for four hours, and also took the unusual step of suggesting that, were they able to nominate one, the runner-up would have been Desai's novel.

Coetzee, who had not been present in person at the awards banquet in 1983, was absent, too, on 25 October 1999, although his editor at Secker & Warburg, Geoff Mulligan, read a prepared acceptance statement on his behalf (his agent, Bruce Hunter, later confirmed that Coetzee had a prior commitment to teach for the full week in Chicago). In his statement, Coetzee called the prize 'the greatest literary prize in the English speaking world', praised his fellow nominees, and declared himself 'honoured' to win (Linklater). Later, he was quoted – in an article by Ong Sor Fern, in Singapore's *Straits Times* – saying that he hoped that his novel 'at least carries the impression of sincerity'. This typically suggestive comment draws attention, of course, to the novel's performance – the fact that the novel is itself a performance of a particular voice, and narrative perspective. Its complex performance of sincerity made it amenable, however, to numerous interpretations, as the previous chapter suggested. Announcing the award of the Booker Prize, the chair of judges, Gerald Kaufman (a British Labour Party MP), stated that *Disgrace* was 'in a sense a millennial book taking us through the 20th century and the shift away from white Western domination' (Lockerbie). In other words, it was amenable to a universalist reading eager to construct it, despite its apparent realism, as in part allegorical, or at least suggestive of conditions found more globally than in South Africa alone.

Alongside Kaufman and Natasha Walter, the other judges were Scottish writer Shena Mackay, academic and journalist John Sutherland, and Boyd Tonkin, the literary editor of the British *Independent* newspaper. Tonkin was quoted the next day having described the novel as 'grim but fantastically well done', both 'a profoundly political book' and 'also a beautifully sustained prose poem' (Walsh). Tonkin himself expanded on this in a piece in the *Independent* several days later, confessing to having felt a qualm in recommending a novel with 'so little reconciliation'. The comment came in a piece entitled 'Where Are The Black Voices From South Africa?', which notes that *Disgrace* was soon to be joined in print by several other narratives of 'the anguish of South Africa's white tribe' (including new titles by Nadine Gordimer, Breyten Breytenbach and Marlene van Niekerk), but that little attention was being given to new black writers. The timing of this article might be taken as an implicit critique of the growing success of Coetzee's novel – though it did little to halt the plaudits. Tonkin had occasion to report on another significant prize awarded to Coetzee for *Disgrace* some months later, when it was announced that the novel had again beaten Rushdie, this time to win the Commonwealth Writers' Prize. *Disgrace* had already been named the best book from the African region, but claimed the overall award in April 2000, at a ceremony in New Delhi. It was doubtless a bittersweet moment for Rushdie, who had made his first return visit to India since the fatwa issued against him in Iran in 1989. He may have been gracious in defeat, but he chided Coetzee's novel in an article that appeared in South African newspapers in May, in which he suggested that the novel failed to illuminate the dystopic world it so convincingly sketched.

Film

Adapting for film or other media novels as complex in structure and narrative perspective as Coetzee's tend to be, is not an easy task. Coetzee himself comments in *Doubling the Point* on the difficulties involved, suggesting that Marion Hänsel's adaptation of *In the Heart of the Country* (filmed as *Dust*, 1985) failed to retain the novel's sequence divisions or pacing, suffering as a result. He noted that he had, in conversations with several prospective directors of mooted adaptations of his novels, 'pleaded for voice-over and in general for the independence of the voice', usually to no avail: 'Even if one encounters a director who is cautiously sympathetic', Coetzee noted, producers and funders, those 'who claim to know what the public will and won't take', were always less understanding: 'It's a wretched state of affairs. Any words on the sound track besides lip-synchronized dialogue are branded as "literary" and therefore old-fashioned. The irony is, doing the narration through dialogue keeps film tied to stage drama. It makes sound film more primitive than silent film' (*DP*, p. 60).

Unfortunately, this is exactly what has happened with the film of *Disgrace*, adapted for the screen and co-produced by Anna-Maria Monticelli, and directed by her husband, Steve Jacobs (both are Australian). It was filmed in South Africa and Australia (some of the Cape Town scenes were filmed in Sydney), was in post-production in 2007, and screened at a number of international film festivals in 2008. It premiered in South Africa at the National Arts Festival in Grahamstown (appropriately enough) in July 2009, and released in several markets later in the year. The filmmakers told an academic audience at a conference in Australia in early 2009 that the difficult economics of the film market militated against the use of voiceover, and the result is that viewers have limited access to the thoughts of David Lurie – played by John Malkovich. There is an attempt to suggest David's focalization – for example, viewers do not see what David does not see in the attack scenes, and consequently share David's uncertainty about what exactly happened to Lucy (played in the film by South African actress Jessica Haines). At times, the loss of David's focalization means the film loses nuance, battling to convey the novel's sometimes ironic tone. For example, in the scene in which David arrives at the

Isaacs home in George and meets Melanie's younger sister, Desiree, the meeting in the film (recognizably *not* filmed in George) has none of the frisson it does, for David, in the novel (in which he imagines what it would be like to sleep with both sisters). Those viewers familiar with the novel, and with its locations, might incidentally also object that its rural scenes were filmed not in the Eastern Cape, but, because the film crews needed to be within two hours' drive of facilities in Cape Town, in the Cedarberg area north of Cape Town (an area that looks very little like Lower Albany). Grahamstown, too, is less obviously modelled on a Georgian English town in the film than it appears in reality (with all of the connotations of cultural affiliation and disjunction, on which the novel draws implicitly).

The film makes good use of diegetic music throughout – in other words, we hear music emanating from identifiable sources within the world of the film. David and Soraya hear music meant to signify 'Africa' through the window of the room in which they have their encounter; there is pop music in Melanie's apartment; and we hear opera on the stereo during a scene in David's car. Each of these instances assists characterization, though occasionally such aural cues seem to go beyond anything suggested in the novel, as when the 'yammer of a radio' (p. 73) in the Shaws' home, becomes, in the film, a recognizably *Afrikaans*-language radio station. This, while not implausible, seems out of keeping with the symbolic freight of the name 'Shaw', as suggested in Chapter 2.

The film also uses non-diegetic music to suggest the chamber opera forming in David's mind: during the opening credits, we hear the beginnings of a choral piece; this recurs as David drives back to Cape Town from the Eastern Cape; and it takes shape as a finished piece, a lush setting of a Byron poem for solo voice and orchestral accompaniment, in the closing minutes of the film and during the final credits. (The piece was commissioned from composer Graeme Koehne, and is performed by the Adelaide Symphony Orchestra.) The poem is Byron's 'She walks in beauty'. In the film, David quotes it to Bev during the scene in which they sleep together (corresponding to the end of Chapter 17 in the novel), and is also shown singing the line in a scene in which he plucks the banjo (in the novel, the end of Chapter 20). The poem is, however, to my knowledge neither quoted nor alluded to in the novel, and its use seems in fact to be unfaithful to the novel's suggestion about the shape and implications of David's changing conception of his project. In the novel, the chamber opera comes to feature Teresa's voice more prominently than Byron's, and the poem which is set to music in the film is, given what David's opera becomes, perhaps awkwardly about the objectification of female beauty in a male poetic voice.

There are several other deviations from the novel, mostly omissions or additions. There is, for example, no scene in the film in which David recognizes Soraya in Central Cape Town: rather, she terminates the arrangement in the first encounter the viewer sees, after David leaves a gift with her payment. David does not burst in on his replacement (Dr Otto), as in the film, so the viewer does not see the poster of Superman being 'berated' by Lois Lane, as in the novel (p. 177). Instead, the film shows a poster of the Romantic poet Percy Shelley, in David's office, before the hearing; Shelley was famously expelled from his Oxford college for promoting atheism, and carries appropriate connotations of rebellion and expulsion (although he is not obviously alluded to in the novel).

While such differences can indicate something about the difficulties inherent in mediating a work of literature whose complexity and very meaning begins at the level of narrative focalization, restricted narrative perspective and voice, into a medium that ostensibly demands externalization of narrative (except through the kind of voiceover to which Coetzee alludes in his references to adaptations of the novels), it is perhaps more interesting and more productive for the purposes of this book to speculate about the kind of life that the film of *Disgrace* may have in the world, and how that life may bear on the book. Certainly, people who have not read the novel will view the film. What will the film appear to be about for such viewers? It will seem, perhaps, to be about a middle-aged professor who is dismissed from his job for his affair with a student, and who gets burned in an attack in which his lesbian daughter is raped. The man helps to dispose of the bodies of euthanized dogs, returns home to find his house has been burgled, and finally returns to the area in which his daughter farms to find she has reached an accommodation with a community that protects one of the men who raped her.

This description oversimplifies the narrative of the film, but it suggests that the film is fairly faithful to the novel's plot – if not to its voice and rhetorical self-reflexivity. Monticelli was quoted in *Filmmaker South Africa* in July 2007 as saying that the 'most important thing' for her, as the writer, was that she 'not bastardise the book'. Apart from the unfortunate biological metaphor (in a context in which metaphors of legitimacy and miscegenation are never without racial and political implications), this comment suggests a dedication to fidelity that appears to have been inter-preted solely on the level of plot. My suggestion, in other words, is that the film of *Disgrace* offers a narrative of white South Africans' experience of life under majority rule that does not sufficiently complicate its narrative focalization, or convey the ironies inherent in that focalization in the novel; the film thus runs the risk, both with local and global audiences, of reinforcing tropes of black peril and white panic that the novel, in its complexity, seeks always to challenge.

The film has little choice in this regard, one might argue: it is impossible for it to delay (or avoid) directly indicating the race of particular characters, for example. The attackers are clearly black from the first moment they appear on screen; Soraya is Malay, and Melanie is coloured. Similarly, although some readers might miss the fact that the doctor who attends to David at the clinic after the attack is 'a young Indian woman' (p. 101), this is more immediately noticeable in the film. The film does, however, both under- and overplay race in peculiar ways. It does not have a black actor portray the chair of the disciplinary panel, so failing to capitalize on parallels with the TRC. And it introduces dialogue, in the performance of *Sunset at the Globe Salon* that David attends in the final Cape Town section, which seems unusually racially loaded: in the novel, the reader learns that the salon owner has mentioned an ultimatum from the landlord (p. 193); in the film, he delivers a tirade against the landlord as a 'savage, savage Indian', and threatens to make 'an exploding onion bhaji'.

The film ends not with David giving up Driepoot to be euthanized, but transposes this scene with that in the novel in which David parks his vehicle and walks towards Lucy's house, watching her tend her garden before she notices him. Lucy's smallholding is, at the end of the film, a lush plot with abundant flowers and vegetables; Lucy invites David in for tea, and the camera pulls back in an extreme long shot that manages to emphasize both the smallness of the house in the vast, desolate (Cedarberg) landscape, but also to linger lovingly on a vision of the pastoral – a vision in which there appears to be considerably more hope than many discern at the end of the novel. Clearly, this is a more cheerful or promising ending, certainly an emotionally less draining one, than would have been the case had the film closed with David bearing a dog to its death. But this choice underlines the fact that this is a deeply filmically conventional adaptation. Ironically, this has not, however, meant that it has fared any better in negotiating the economics of the international film marketplace at a difficult moment in the midst of a global recession. At the time of writing, the film had only been on limited release in some markets although it did win the International Critics' Award (FIPRESCI) at the 2008 Toronto International Film Festival. Coetzee's verdict on the film is not known.

5

Discussion Questions, Glossary and Further Reading

Questions and Topics for Discussion

1. What do you make of Lucy's speculation that what happens to her is 'the price one has to pay for staying on' (p. 158)? Do you understand why elements in the South African (ANC) government, as well as some Afrikaner intellectuals, objected to this formulation? How serious is Lucy? Does anything in the novel explain her attitude? Does her attitude change?

2. The writer and academic Elleke Boehmer remains unconvinced that Coetzee's novel engages sensitively with the reality of gender violence in South Africa (or in any country in a similar position), and is troubled by the fate the novel seems to imagine for Lucy. 'How', Boehmer asks, 'can we speak of atonement if it entails that women as ever assume the generic pose of suffering in silence or, as does Lucy, of gestating peacefully in her garden? Is reconciliation with a history of violence possible if the woman – the white Lucy, or indeed the black wife of Petrus – is as ever biting her lip?' (2002 p. 350). How would you respond to Boehmer's criticism and concerns?

3. How significant is it that so much of the narrative is focalized through David Lurie or presented in dialogue? Try rewriting a portion of a chapter from the perspective of an omniscient third-person narration (not a limited one) and without focalization, or try focalizing through Petrus, Bev, or Lucy. If you're in a class or in a reading group, try reading different versions of the same passage to each other; what insights does this exercise give into Coetzee's choice of David as focalizer? Is this exercise problematic, in that it invites you to give a voice to or to represent 'others' when this is perhaps precisely the presumption (David's to speak for others) that the novel suggests the reader might interrogate?

4. How relevant do you think possible parallels between the Truth and Reconciliation Commission and David's disciplinary hearing are? How do you account for the manner in which David behaves before the panel? How do you explain Farodia Rassool's particular objections to David's answers?

5. What do you think are the reasons for Coetzee's narrative being reticent about naming the race of characters for so long? Do you feel that having, or not having, access to knowledge about racial markers and indicators in South Africa aids or hinders your reading of the novel?

6. Consider the significance of Lucy's refusal to call the smallholding a farm (p. 200)? How do you interpret this? Do you think Petrus would have the same qualms about using the term to refer to his parcel of land? Why (not)?

7. How do you explain Petrus's reluctance to entertain the idea of turning Pollux over to the police or removing him from the smallholding? How is Petrus's understanding of family and kin characterized in the novel? Do we learn much about Petrus or his family through anyone's perspective but David's?

8. If, as the critic Derek Attridge points out, the opposite of disgrace is not grace, but honour (2004, pp. 177–8), what – if anything – might end David's state of disgrace? How do you understand the operation of grace in the novel, if indeed you see it as being present? Is disgrace a state shared with any other characters? How does David think animals feel or sense disgrace?

9. Another critic, Michael Marais, argues that '*Disgrace* ... proposes a renegotiation of interpersonal relations which would install respect for the otherness of other beings and thereby obviate the possibility of violence' (2001, p. 38). Do you agree? If so, why? If not, why not?

10. How does Coetzee's depiction of South Africa in the years immediately after the transition to a post-Apartheid social order compare with other fictional treatments from the same period? You might like to consider Nadine Gordimer's *The House Gun* (1998) and Zoë Wicomb's *David's Story* (2000), in particular. You could also think about Coetzee's uses of complex narrative perspective and layers of irony in representing or alluding to violence and testimony, comparing *Disgrace* with Antjie Krog's famous creative non-fiction account of reporting on the Truth and Reconciliation Commission, *Country of My Skull* (1998).

11. How does Coetzee's engagement with history differ from that of black South African writers of fiction in the same period? You might like to consider *Disgrace* alongside, for example, Zakes Mda's novel *The Heart of Redness* (2000). How do both novels treat the history of the Xhosa people and conditions in the present-day South African province of the Eastern Cape?

12. In a review of South African poet and artist Breyten Breytenbach's memoir, *Dog Heart* (also published in 1999), Coetzee suggests that Breytenbach's 'ethical philosophy' is chiefly concerned with two things: 'bastardy and nomadism'. Coetzee comments: 'Just as the bastard sheds his self and enters into unprecedented mixture with the other, so the nomad uproots himself from the old, comfortable dwelling place to follow the animals ... or the figures of his imagination, into an uncertain future' (*Stranger Shores*, p. 312). How suggestive is this comment for reading *Disgrace*? How does the novel foreground both issues? You might like to read Breytenbach's book and to compare it to *Disgrace*; what differences are there in the books' treatments of race and their representation of dogs?

13. What is the role of the chamber opera in *Disgrace*? Can we interpret David's changing attitude towards it as a reflection by Coetzee on the nature of art?

14. Peter D. McDonald, who writes perceptively about the category of the 'literary' in South Africa, suggests that *Disgrace*'s 'charged story, artful rhetoric, dense allusiveness, and studied refusal to moralize' all contribute to 'diverse effects' that make 'difficult, even excessive demands on its readers' (2002, p. 330). Expand on the nature of these difficulties as proposed by McDonald. Do you agree that they are excessive? Has reading *Disgrace* made you think differently about the activity of reading in general?

15. In an essay entitled 'The Harms of Pornography', published in *Giving Offense* (1996), Coetzee speculates about the possibility of a 'male writer-pornographer' who might offer 'an account of power that ... does not close the book on desire'. Were this 'hypothetical account' to be attempted in fiction rather than 'theory', and to share 'a thematics with pornography', in other words perhaps including representations or discussions of 'torture, abasement, acts of cruelty', Coetzee wonders whether anything would prevent it from being labelled exploitative, distasteful, or pornographic (p. 72). Is this hypothetical account in any way like what Coetzee attempts in *Disgrace*? Does the possibility that it might be suggest we ought to read the novel's representation of violence and exploitation differently?

16. *Disgrace* is an extremely allusive novel: David Lurie makes reference to a number of works of European literature. What is the purpose of these allusions? Does knowing their sources – see the glossary in this chapter – change the way you read the novel? How important is it to understand the words and phrases drawn from South African languages?

Glossary

Page references are to the Secker & Warburg and Vintage editions of *Disgrace*.

Abbreviations: A = Afrikaans; F = French; G = German; I = Italian; L = Latin; X = Xhosa (strictly *isi*Xhosa); SAE denotes common usage in South African English (including composite forms, or non-English words commonly used by first-language English-speakers in some parts of South Africa).

aanhangers (p. 208): hangers-on, followers (A).
Ag (p. 24): 'Oh', general expression used in multiple circumstances (A).
Aliter (p. 179): 'other' or 'otherwise' (L).
baas en Klaas (p. 116): (A) master (*baas*) and servant (*Klaas* stands in as a representative name).
basta (p. 89): enough! (I).
boervrou (p. 60): 'farmer's wife' or 'farmer woman' (A).
boytjie (p. 81): little boy (boy + Afrikaans suffix indicating the diminutive); a term of endearment or affection, also used of animals (A, SAE).

buchu (p. 71): a plant (species of *Barosma*) traditionally used for tea as well as medicinally; the name is likely of Khoisan origin.

bywoner (p. 204): (A) sharecropper, tenant farmer (also SAE).

CASUALTIES (p. 101): Emergency room; Accident and Emergency section of a hospital (SAE).

Che vuol dir questa solitudine immensa? Ed io, che sono? (p. 213): (I) 'What is the meaning of this great solitude? And I, who am I?'; a quotation from translation of 'Canto Notturno di un Pastore Errante dell'Asia', a poem by the Italian writer Giacomo Leopardi (1798–1837).

chuchotantes (p. 101): (F) lit. whisperings (by women).

contadina (p. 181): (I) female peasants or farmers.

contra naturam (p. 190): (L) contrary or against nature or the course of nature.

coup de grâce (p. 95): (F) lit. 'stroke of grace', fig. finishing stroke, that which puts an end to something.

coup de main (p. 31): (F) lit. a stroke of the hand, fig. a vigorous attack with the intention of gaining a position.

dagga (p. 60): common name for hemp, *Cannabis sativa*, used as a narcotic (also used of indigenous plants of the genus *Leonotis*, 'wild dagga'), probably derived from Khoikhoi and Nama words (A, SAE).

das ewig Weibliche (p. 218): (G) 'the eternal feminine', or 'eternal woman', quotation from Part Two of *Faust*, by the German author Johann Wolfgang von Goethe (1749–1832), where it is sung in praise of the Virgin Mary by a chorus of spirits who welcome Faust to heaven.

Doctor Khumalo (p. 128): Theophilus 'Doctor' Khumalo (b. 1967). South African professional soccer (in Britain 'football') star (retired), long a star player for famous Soweto-based team Kaizer Chiefs.

donga (p. 98): word originally of Nguni origin (X, isiZulu), commonly used in A and SAE to refer to an eroded gully or dry riverbed.

Driepoot (p. 215): (A) literally 'three-legs' or 'three-feet'.

duenna (p. 39): from the Spanish *dueña*; formerly 'duenna', term for a mistress or married woman, originally also older woman companion or chaperone.

duiker (p. 73): (A) small antelope; word derived from the Dutch 'to dive' (relating to the movements of the animal in the bush). The name is used in A and SAE of several species in the subfamily *Cephalophinae*.

Du musst dein Leben ändern (p. 209): (G) literally 'you must change your life', a line from the poem 'Archaic Torso of Apollo' by Rainer Maria Rilke (1875–1926). Coetzee reviewed a volume of translations of Rilke poems, including this one, in 1999 (see *Stranger Shores* p. 71).

Eid (p. 5): Arabic, common abbreviation for Eid al-Adha, the 'feast of sacrifice', an Islamic holy day or canonical festival associated with commemorating the direction to Ibrahim to sacrifice his son, Ismael.

eingewurzelt (p. 117): (G) deep-rooted or deep-seated.

entr'actes (p. 184): (F) interval between the acts of a play or performance.

Faro (p. 87): from (I) and (F) for 'Pharaoh', a card game involving betting on the order in which cards will be taken from the top of a pack.

Hamba! (p. 92): (X) 'Go away!'

handlanger (p. 136): assistant or helper (Dutch, also A); also colloquial, for follower (SAE).

harijan (p. 146): from the Sanskrit *harijana*, a person (*jana*) graced by the Hindu god Vishnu (*Hari*). Gandhi applied the term, intended as empowering, to the *dalits* or so-called Untouchables in India.

Hypnagogic (p. 192): inducing or leading to sleep.

inamorata (pp. 44, 189): (I) mistress, female lover.

J'accuse (p. 40): 'I accuse' (F), a reference to Émile Zola's January 1898 open letter accusing the French state of anti-Semitism in the Dreyfus affair.

jou dom meid! (p. 192): (A) literally 'you stupid maid!', but with particular pejorative connotations, and implicitly addressed to a young black or coloured female (not necessarily a servant).

Kaaps (pp. 24, 191): literally 'of the Cape' (A), but specifically related to coloured or Malay version of Afrikaans, or culture, associated with Cape Town or the Western Cape.

kaffir (p. 140): derived from Arabic for 'infidel' or unbeliever (non-Muslim), once in widespread use in the colonial period to refer to black Africans; in South Africa in the twentieth century a derogatory word for black South Africans, and in post-Apartheid South Africa highly inflammatory and offensive.

kombi (pp. 59, 64, 70, 99, 109, 142, 144, 147, 153, etc.): a van or minibus, originally specifically a model manufactured by Volkswagen, popular in South Africa as a passenger or goods vehicle (or both) (SAE).

la donna è mobile (p. 3): (I) 'women are fickle'; an aria from Italian composer Giuseppe Verdi's opera *Rigoletto* (1851).

la mal'aria (p. 186): (I) 'bad air', origin of English 'malaria'.

ländliche (p. 113): (G) bucolically, rurally.

lösen (p. 142): (G) verb 'to solve', to implement or cause a solution (literally or figuratively).

Lösung (pp. 142, 218): (G) a solution, both metaphorical and literal (liquid); echoes *Endlösung*, the Third Reich's so-called 'final solution' of mass extermination of European Jewry.

luxe et volupté (p. 1): (F) 'luxury and pleasure', variation of 'Luxe, calme, et volupté' in the poem 'Invitation au voyage' by Charles Baudelaire (1821–67).

My gats (p. 24): literally something like 'my hole' (A); homophonic exclamation avoiding the blasphemy of *My god(s)* – spelt the same in Afrikaans as in English – and used as a general exclamation of alarm or surprise.

masa (p. 71): version of *amasi* (X) and *maas* (A): cultured sour or fermented milk.

mealies (p. 60): (SAE) maize, from *mielie* (A).

Meerlust (p. 12): Dutch for desire (*lust*) for the sea (*meer*), understood too in Afrikaans (in which desire or vitality is *lus*); the name of a well-known wine estate. It can be heard in English as a homonym for *mere lust*, adding to its ironic use in the novel.

Mio Byron (pp. 182–3, 185): 'My Byron' (I).

Mncedisi (p. 200): male first-name (X) meaning 'the helper'.

Molo (p. 201): (X) 'Hello' (singular).

muti (p. 145): from the isiZulu word *umuthi* for plant, tree, or medicine, used widely in South Africa (incl. X, SAE) for medicine, or traditional medicine (especially, but not necessarily only that with which supernatural powers might be associated, in which case can be consumed, or a talisman or charm).

Nqabayakhe (p. 200): male first-name (X) meaning 'her fortress'.

nom de commerce (p. 8): (F) pseudonym or alias used for business purposes.

Omnis gens quaecumque se in se perficere vult (p. 194): (L) roughly translates as 'each nation, whatsoever it is, wants to perfect itself in itself'.

Oom (p. 71): Uncle (A); widely used as term of respect for any older man, not necessarily related.

overall (pp. 61, 63): coverall, boiler suit (SAE).

Ovral (p. 198): trade name for an oral contraceptive.

paysan (p. 117): (F) peasant.

psychopomp (p. 146): guide of souls to the afterlife; in Jungian psychology, link between the unconscious and the ego.

Qu'est devenu ce front poli, ces cheveux blonds, sourcils voûtés? (p. 65): (F) 'what became of this polished forehead, blond hair, arched eyebrows?', quotation from the poem 'Regrets of the Belle Heaulmiére', a meditation on the ravages of time on a celebrated beauty, by the fifteenth-century French poet François Villon (b. c1431).

regina et imperatrix (p. 135): Queen and Empress (L), titles in use throughout the British Empire for Queen Victoria.

reliquie (p. 181): from (L) for remains or relics.

Schadenfreude (p. 42): (G) delight in the misfortunes of others.

sotto voce (p. 56): (I) in a low or subdued voice.

Sunt lacrimae rerum, et mentem mortalia tangunt (p. 162): from Virgil's *Aeneid* (L), from a passage in which Aeneas, seeing a depiction of the Trojan War in a temple mural in Carthage, feels with his whole mind and soul the futility of warfare and suffering.

SAPPI (p. 69): abbreviation for South African Pulp and Paper Industries Limited, a paper and pulp-producing firm founded in South Africa in 1936, and now a global operation.

stoep (p. 59): porch, veranda, or raised platform along the front or around the sides of a house (A, SAE).

Tante (p. 71): Aunt (as for Oom, not necessarily related).

tessitura (p. 81): (I) texture; in music also refers to part of a melody containing most of its tones.

Tretchikoff (p. 128): Russian-born South African painter Vladimir

Tretchikoff (1913–2006), whose paintings, often labelled 'kitsch' by critics, were immensely popular internationally, particularly in the 1960s and 1970s. The most famous of these is 'Green Lady', also known as 'Chinese Girl', a portrait of a woman 'Discreet Escorts' (*Disgrace*, p. 7) might well have called 'exotic'.

Vedi l'anime di color cui vinse l'ira (p. 209): a quotation from Canto VII of the *Inferno* (by the medieval Italian poet Dante Alighieri, c. 1265–1321), in which Dante is directed to 'see the souls of those overcome with anger'.

Some other unattributed quotations and allusions (in English):

'does not belong to her alone' (p. 16): Biblical reference (1 Corinthians 7: 4); David adapts the quotations, which refers in the original to relations between husband and wife.

'From fairest creatures we desire increase ... that thereby beauty's rose might never die' (p. 16): from Sonnet 1 in Shakespeare's *Sonnets* (1609).

'Blest be the infant babe. No outcast he. Blest be the babe' (p. 46): a variation on lines from Wordsworth's *The Prelude*, Book Two (1850 text, lines 232, 241).

'Sooner murder an infant in its cradle than nurse unacted desires' (p. 69): from Blake's *The Marriage of Heaven and Hell* (c. 1790–3), specifically 'The Proverbs of Hell' (Plate 10, line 7).

'Mad, bad, and dangerous to know' (p. 77): attributed to Lady Caroline Lamb, who had a short-lived affair with Byron, to whom the quote refers.

'Though the heart be still as loving and the moon be still as bright' (p. 120): lines from Byron's poem 'So, We'll Go No More A Roving'.

'*because we are too menny*' (p. 146): from the suicide note of Jude's eldest child, in Thomas Hardy's *Jude the Obscure* (1895), Part 6, ch. 2.

'how are the mighty fallen' (p. 167): The Old Testament figure David's lament (uttered three times) over the deaths of Saul and Jonathan in the King James version of the Bible (1 Samuel 1: 19, 25, 27).

'And ye shall be as one flesh' (p. 169): Biblical reference, to 1 Corinthians 6: 16.

'Let both be tied till one shall have expired' (p. 185): from Byron's *Don Juan*, Canto III, stanza 7.

'The young in one another's arms ... No country, this, for old men' (p. 190): quotation from and allusion to the first two lines of W. B. Yeats's poem, 'Sailing to Byzantium' (1927).

'Whatever does not kill me makes me stronger' (p. 191): from initial chapter of Friedrich Nietzsche's *Twilight of the Idols* (1895).

'A fair field full of folk' (p. 192): from the 'Prologue' of Langland's *Piers Plowman*, in which Will falls asleep on the Malvern hills and dreams of a field of people arranged according to their estate.

'Like a dog' (p. 205): reference to the final sentences of Franz Kafka's *The Trial* (1925).

Further Reading

Works by J. M. Coetzee

Novels and other Fiction

Dusklands. Johannesburg: Ravan, 1974. Harmondsworth: Penguin, 1982. New York: Penguin, 1985.

In the Heart of the Country. London: Secker & Warburg; New York: Harper & Row (as *From the Heart of the Country*), 1977. Johannesburg: Ravan, 1978.

Waiting for the Barbarians. Johannesburg: Ravan; London: Secker & Warburg, 1980. New York: Penguin, 1982.

Life & Times of Michael K. Johannesburg: Ravan; London: Secker & Warburg; New York: Viking, 1983.

Foe. Johannesburg: Ravan; London: Secker & Warburg, 1986. New York: Viking, 1987.

Age of Iron. London: Secker & Warburg; New York: Random House, 1990.

The Master of Petersburg. London: Secker & Warburg; New York: Viking, 1994.

Disgrace. London: Secker & Warburg; New York: Viking, 1999.

The Lives of Animals, ed. & intro. Amy Gutmann. Princeton: Princeton University Press, 1999. London: Profile, 2001 (without accompanying responses).

Elizabeth Costello: Eight Lessons. London: Secker & Warburg; New York: Viking, 2003.

Slow Man. London: Secker & Warburg; New York: Viking, 2005.

Diary of a Bad Year. London: Harvill Secker; New York: Viking, 2007.

Fictionalized Memoir

Boyhood: Scenes from Provincial Life. London: Secker & Warburg; New York: Viking, 1997; London: Vintage, 1998.

Youth. London: Secker & Warburg; New York: Viking, 2002.

Summertime. London: Harvill Secker; New York: Viking, 2009.

Essays and Criticism

'The Novel Today'. *Upstream*. 1988, v.6: 1. 2–5.

White Writing: On the Culture of Letters in South Africa. New Haven: Yale University Press, 1988.

Doubling the Point: Essays and Interviews, ed. David Attwell. Cambridge, MA: Harvard University Press, 1992.

Giving Offense: Essays on Censorship. Chicago: University of Chicago Press, 1996.

Stranger Shores: Essays 1986–1999. London: Secker & Warburg; New York: Viking (subtitled *Literary Essays 1986–1999*), 2001.

Inner Workings: Literary Essays 2000–2005. London: Harvill Secker; New York: Viking, 2007.

Interviews

'All Autobiography is *Autre*-biography' (2002). With David Attwell. In *Selves in Question: Interviews on South African Auto/biography*. Judith Lütge Coullie, Stephan Meyer, *et al*. (eds). Honolulu: University of Hawai'i Press, 2006. 213–17.

Doubling the Point: Essays and Interviews. With David Attwell. Cambridge, MA: Harvard University Press, 1992.

'Two Interviews with J.M. Coetzee, 1983 and 1987'. With Tony Morphet. *TriQuarterly* 69 (1987), 454–64. Special issue: *South Africa: New Writing, Photographs and Art*. Jane Taylor and David Bunn (eds).

Other Primary Material

Books

Blake, William. *Blake: Complete Writings*. Geoffrey Keynes (ed.). Oxford: Oxford University Press, 1972.

Breytenbach, Breyten. *Dog Heart: A Memoir*. London: Faber; New York: Harcourt Brace, 1999.

Butler, Guy. *Richard Gush of Salem*. Cape Town: Maskew Miller, 1982.

Byron, George Gordon, Lord. *Byron*. Jerome J. McGann (ed.). [Oxford Authors.] Oxford: Oxford University Press, 1986.

Gordimer, Nadine. *The House Gun*. London: Bloomsbury; New York: Farrar, Straus and Giroux, 1998.

Krog, Antjie. *Country of My Skull*. Johannesburg: Random House, 1998. London: Vintage, 1999.

Mda, Zakes. *The Heart of Redness*. Cape Town: Oxford University Press (South Africa), 2000. New York: Farrar, Straus and Giroux, 2002.

Wicomb, Zoë. *David's Story*. Cape Town: Kwela Books, 2000. New York: Feminist Press at the City University of New York, 2001.

Wordsworth, William. *The Prelude: A Parallel Text* (1805/6 & 1850). J. C. Maxwell (ed.). Harmondsworth: Penguin, 1972.

Wu, Duncan (ed.). *Romanticism: An Anthology*. 2nd edn. Malden, MA, and Oxford: Blackwell, 1998.

Films

Dust. Dir. Marion Hänsel. Prod. Daska Films, Flach Film, France 3 Cinéma, Man's Films, Ministerie van de Vlaamse Gemeenschap, Ministère de la Communauté Française de Belgique. 1985.

Disgrace. Dir. Steve Jacobs. Prod. Fortissimo Films, Sherman Films, Whitest Pouring Films, Wild Strawberries. 2008.

Select Secondary Material

Biography

Frängsmyr, Töre (ed.). *Le Prix Nobel. The Nobel Prizes 2003*. Stockholm: Nobel Foundation, 2004.

Selected Criticism

Attridge, Derek. 'Age of Bronze, State of Grace: Music and Dogs in Coetzee's *Disgrace*'. *Novel*. 2000, v.34: 1. 98–121.

—— . *J.M. Coetzee and the Ethics of Reading: Literature in the Event*. Chicago: University of Chicago Press, 2004.

Attwell, David. *J.M. Coetzee: South Africa and the Politics of Writing*. Berkeley: University of California Press, 1993.

—— . 'Race in *Disgrace*'. *Interventions*. 2002, v.4: 3. 331–41.

—— . 'J. M. Coetzee and South Africa: 'Thoughts on the Social Life of Fiction'. *English Academy Review: Southern African Journal of English Studies*. 2004, v.21: 3. 105–17.

—— . 'The Life and Times of Elizabeth Costello: J.M. Coetzee and the Public Sphere', in Poyner (ed.), *J.M. Coetzee and the Idea of the Public Intellectual*. 2006. 25–41.

Barnard, Rita. 'Coetzee's Country Ways'. *Interventions*. 2002, v.4: 3. 384–94.

—— . '*Disgrace* and the South African Pastoral'. *Contemporary Literature*. 2003, v.44: 2. 199–204.

—— . *Apartheid and Beyond: South African Writers and the Politics of Place*. New York and Oxford: Oxford University Press, 2007.

Boehmer, Elleke. 'Not Saying Sorry, not Speaking Pain: Gender Implications in *Disgrace*'. *Interventions*. 2002, v.4: 3. 342–51.

Cornwell, Gareth. '*Disgrace*land: History and the Humanities in Frontier Country'. *English in Africa*. 2003, v.30: 2. 43–68.

DelConte, Matt. 'A Further Study of Present Tense Narration: The Absentee Narratee and Four-Wall Present Tense in Coetzee's *Waiting for the Barbarians* and *Disgrace*'. *Journal of Narrative Technique*. 2007, v.37: 3. 427–46.

Easton, Kai. 'Coetzee's *Disgrace*: Byron in Italy and the Eastern Cape c. 1820'. *Journal of Commonwealth Literature*. 2007, v.42: 3. 113–30.

Gaylard, Gerald. 'Disgraceful Metafiction: Intertextuality in the Post-colony'. *Journal of Literary Studies*. 2005, v.21: 3&4. 315–37.

Graham, Lucy. '"Yes, I am giving him up": sacrificial responsibility and likeness with dogs in J. M. Coetzee's recent fiction'. *Scrutiny2*. 2002, v.7: 1. 4–15.

——. 'Reading the Unspeakable: Rape in J.M. Coetzee's *Disgrace*'. *Journal of Southern African Studies*. 2003, v.29: 2. 433–44.

Head, Dominic. 'A Belief in Frogs: J.M. Coetzee's Enduring Faith in Fiction', in Poyner (ed.), *J.M. Coetzee and the Idea of the Public Intellectual*. 2006. 100–17.

Jolly, Rosemary. 'Going to the Dogs: Humanity in J.M. Coetzee's *Disgrace, The Lives of Animals*, and South Africa's Truth and Reconciliation Commission', in Poyner (ed.), *J.M. Coetzee and the Idea of the Public Intellectual*. 2006. 148–71.

Lamb, Jonathan. 'Modern Metamorphoses and Disgraceful Tales'. *Critical Inquiry*. 2001, v.28: 1. 133–66.

Marais, Michael. 'The Possibility of Ethical Action: J. M. Coetzee's *Disgrace*'. *Scrutiny2*. 2000, v.5: 1. 57–63.

——. 'Very Morbid Phenomena: "Liberal Funk", the "Lucy-syndrome" and J. M. Coetzee's *Disgrace*'. *Scrutiny2*. 2001, v.6: 1. 32–8.

——. 'J. M. Coetzee's *Disgrace* and the Task of the Imagination'. *Journal of Modern Literature*. 2006, v.29: 2. 75–93.

McDonald, Bill. ' "Is it too late to educate the eye?": David Lurie, Richard of St Victor, and "vision as eros" in *Disgrace*', in B. McDonald (ed.), *Encountering* Disgrace. 2009. 64–92.

—— (ed.). *Encountering* Disgrace: *Reading and Teaching Coetzee's Novel*. Rochester, NY: Camden House, 2009.

McDonald, Peter D. 'Disgrace Effects'. *Interventions*. 2002, v.4: 3. 321–30.

Pechey, Graham. 'Coetzee's Purgatorial Africa: The Case of *Disgrace*'. *Interventions*. 2002, v.4: 3. 374–83.

Poyner, Jane (ed.), *J.M. Coetzee and the Idea of the Public Intellectual*. Athens, OH: Ohio University Press, 2006.

Rose, Jacqueline. 'Apathy and Accountability: South Africa's Truth and Reconciliation Commission'. *Raritan*. 2002, v.21: 4. 175–95.

Sanders, Mark. *Ambiguities of Witnessing: Literature in the Time of a Truth Commission*. Stanford: Stanford University Press, 2007.

Segall, Kimberly Wedeven. 'Pursuing Ghosts: The Traumatic Sublime in J. M. Coetzee's *Disgrace*'. *Research in African Literatures*. 2005, v.36: 4. 40–54.

Small, Helen. *The Long Life*. Oxford: Oxford University Press, 2007.

Spivak, Gayatri Chakravorty. 'Ethics and Politics in Tagore, Coetzee, and Certain Scenes of Teaching'. *Diacritics*. 2002, v.32: 3–4. 17–31.

Sutcliffe, Patricia Casey. 'Saying it Right in *Disgrace*: David Lurie, *Faust*, and the Romantic Conception of Language', in B. McDonald (ed.), *Encountering* Disgrace. 2009. 173–201.

Wicomb, Zoë. 'Translations in the Yard of Africa'. *Journal of Literary Studies*. 2002, v.18: 3&4. 209–23.

Reviews, Reports, Responses

Attwell, David. 'Coetzee and Post-Apartheid South Africa'. *Journal of Southern African Studies*. (2001), v.27: 4. 865–7.

—— . 'Are children ready for *Disgrace*[?]'. *The Sowetan* [Soweto, Johannesburg]. 26 March 2004. 23.

Bailey, Paul. 'Books: Sex and Other Problems'. *The Independent* [London]. 3 July 1999. 9.

Banville, John. 'Endgame'. *New York Review of Books*. 20 January 2000. 23–25

Battersby, Eileen. 'Vanity Case'. *The Irish Times*. 14 August 1999. 69.

Cheong, Felix. 'A Rare Work of Grace'. *The Straits Times* [Singapore]. 23 October 1999. *Life*. 19.

du Preez, Max. 'It's a disgrace, but the truth is …'. *The Star* [Johannesburg]. 27 January 2000. 18.

du Toit, Albert. 'Finely tuned novel set in new SA'. *Eastern Province Herald* [Port Elizabeth, South Africa]. 11 August 1999. 4.

Gerwel, Jakes. 'Perspektief: Is *dít* die regte beeld van ons nasie?' [Is *this* the right image of our nation?]. *Rapport* [South Africa]. 13 February 2000. 2.

Goldsworthy, Peter. 'Six of the Best'. *Sydney Morning Herald*. 23 October 1999. *Spectrum*. 9.

Gorra, Michael. 'After the Fall'. *New York Times*. 28 November 1999. Section 7. 7.

Hollands, Glenn. 'Sophisticated Award Winner'. *Daily Dispatch* [East London, South Africa]. 20 May 2000. 4.

Hynes, James. 'Sins of the Father'. *Washington Post*. 16 January 2000. *Book World*. X01.

Jackson, Marni. 'Finding redemption through *Disgrace*'. *Globe and Mail* [Canada]. 25 November 2000. D62.

Jaggi, Maya. 'Speak for the Silenced: How does a white write about black lives? Ask their nanny?' *Guardian*. 20 November 1999. Saturday 9.

Klaaste, Aggrey. 'Odious Terre'blanche is a cartoonist's dream'. *The Sowetan* [Soweto, Johannesburg]. 3 April 2000. 9.

Kunkel, Benjamin. 'Appetite for Allegory'. *Village Voice* [New York]. 15–21 December 1999. Archived at <http://www.villagevoice.com/1999-12-14/books/appetiteforallegory/>

Linklater, Alexander. 'Coetzee does a literary double at the Booker'. *The Herald* [Glasgow]. 26 October 1999. 7.

Lockerbie, Catherine. 'Coetzee Wins Booker Prize For Second Time'. *The Scotsman*. 26 October 1999. 3.

Lowry, Elizabeth. 'Like a Dog'. *London Review of Books*. 14 October 1999. 12–14.

Martin, Sandra. 'A post-Apartheid dinosaur'. *Globe and Mail* [Canada]. 2 October 1999. D18.

Morris, Michael. 'Coetzee thinks publicly about new SA'. *Cape Argus* [Cape Town]. 10 August 1999. 16.

Nickson, Keith. 'A Fall From Grace'. *Toronto Star*. 31 October 1999. Sunday, Edition 1. *Entertainment*. np.

Ong Sor Fern. 'No Disgrace as Coetzee wins again'. *Straits Times* [Singapore]. 27 October 1999. *Life*. 3.

Pye, Michael. 'A Bleak Angle'. *The Scotsman*. 26 June 1999. 10.

Rushdie, Salman. 'A Novel that Leaves Us Blindfolded Among History's Rubble'. *The Independent* [Cape Town]. 7 May 2000. 4.

Tonkin, Boyd. 'Where Are The Black Voices From South Africa?'. *The Independent* [London]. 30 October 1999. 10.

—— . 'Coetzee Beats Rushdie To Prize'. *The Independent* [London]. 15 April 2000. 2.

Trapido, Barbara. 'Books: Sensitivity Training with Dogs'. *The Independent* [London]. 4 July 1999. 10.

Walsh, John. 'A Teller of Spare and Haunting Fables that Carry Weight of History'. *The Independent* [London]. 26 October 1999. 5.

Younghusband, Toni. Review of *Disgrace*. *Femina* [South Africa]. September 1999. 148.

General

Adhikari, Mohamed. *Not White Enough, Not Black Enough: Racial Identity in the South African Coloured Community*. Athens: Ohio University Press; Cape Town: Double Storey, 2005.

Beinart, William. *Twentieth-Century South Africa*. 2nd edn. Oxford & New York: Oxford University Press, 2001.

McDonald, Peter D. *The Literature Police: Apartheid Censorship and its Cultural Consequences*. Oxford: Oxford University Press, 2009.

Mostert, Noël. *Frontiers: The Epic of South Africa's Creation and the Tragedy of the Xhosa People*. London: Pimlico, 1993.

Posel, Deborah, and Graeme Simpson (eds). *Commissioning the Past: Understanding South Africa's Truth and Reconciliation Commission*. Johannesburg: Witwatersrand University Press, 2002.

Rosenstein, Neil. *The Lurie Legacy: The House of Davidic Royal Descent*. Bergenfield, NJ: Avotaynu, 2004.

Van der Vlies, Andrew. *South African Textual Cultures: Black, White, Read All Over*. Manchester: Manchester University Press, 2007.

Wicomb, Zoë. 'Shame and identity: the case of the coloured in South Africa', in Derek Attridge and Rosemary Jolly (eds). *Writing South Africa: Literature, Apartheid, and Democracy, 1970–1995*. Cambridge: Cambridge University Press, 1998. 91–107.

Websites

Permanent Secretary, Swedish Academy. 'The Nobel Prize in Literature 2003'. Press release & related links. 2 October 2003. http://nobelprize.org/nobel_prizes/literature/ laureates/2003/press.html.

Filmmaker South Africa. 'You Ought to be in Pictures'. 18 July 2007. www.filmmaker.co.za/print.php?type=A&item_id=921.

Filmmaker South Africa. 'Sold-out Shows for Fortissimo Films'. 14 February 2008. www.filmmaker.co.za/print.php?type=A&item_id=2145.